COLLECTION AGENCY

# HARASSMENT:

## What the Debt Collector Doesn't Want You to Know

# COLLECTION AGENCY
# HARASSMENT:
## What the Debt Collector Doesn't Want You to Know

## BY RICHARD L. DIMAGGIO, JURIS DOCTOR

## THE CONSUMER PRESS

LCCN 2002090110.

Printed in the United States of America

Design by Carol Sawyer of Rose Design

DAD, I MISS YOU.

■

KIM, I LOVE YOU.

■

ANDREW, YOU ARE MY LITTLE SUNSHINE.
YOU HAVE TAUGHT ME HOW TO LOVE
IN WAYS I NEVER IMAGINED.

## ABOUT THE CONSUMER PRESS

The author of this book, Richard DiMaggio, Juris Doctor, founded **The Consumer Press** in 2001, after noting a complete scarcity of presses, written material, and yes, lawyers too, dedicated to you, the consumer. He has been a lawyer for over 10 years, devoting his time and efforts to consumer protection issues. He founded **The Consumer Press** after realizing very few lawyers, let alone lay people, knew the intricacies of consumer issues. The credit industry certainly knows these issues well: They hold seminars and lectures to teach and devise ways to *deceive* the consumer. Books published by **The Consumer Press** help to teach you the tricks and deception that the author has uncovered throughout his decade of litigating against these tyrants. **The Consumer Press** books teach you what the "industry" doesn't want you to know: The tricks, ploys, and brotherhood of lies the collection industry has developed and kept to itself.

After litigating against collection agencies, mortgage companies, and credit reporting agencies for over a decade, the author feels the time has come to put the consumer at the forefront of our credit industry. This is the first in a series of consumer publications. Look for these additional titles:

*Mortgage Fraud: What the Mortgage Industry Doesn't Want You to Know*

*Credit Reporting: What the Credit Reporting Industry Doesn't Want You to Know*

*Auto Finance Fraud: What the Auto Industry Doesn't Want You to Know*

Visit our web site at www.theconsumerpress.com.
Feel free to e-mail us with any and all questions you may have.
We also welcome queries from authors.

# The Consumer Press

# TESTIMONIALS

"One turn of the corner and your life can be changed but your sense of self worth should not. I did not learn what to do when the unexpected occurs in any financial planning seminar or college course. To feel you're being harped on or stomped on by someone who hides behind a phone to squeeze what little you have left is wrong! Rich, your expertise has given me the ability to feel empowered in my financial situation and allowed me to move ahead. I could not put this book down until I finished it. Your birds-eye-view has given me a better sense of the big picture; how I fit in and how the debt harassment does not. Now I've become an even better educated consumer and I now know and feel I am worth much more than the debts I can pay or the debts I still owe.

"Thank you Rich, I owe you in ways I cannot repay!

"Hats off to you!"

*Perla, upstate, NY*

"A great lawyer is like a great mechanic . . . trusting, honest and very hard to find. Rich DiMaggio exemplifies a great lawyer! He has perfected his art and seriously helps people with true honesty in this book."

*Taylor A., Ballston Spa, NY*

"Everyone should have a Richard DiMaggio in their corner. Anyone who has been abused by debt collectors should read what he has to say. . . . Compassionate and a gifted attorney who wasn't afraid to stand and fight."

*Barbara D., Ballston Spa, NY*

"What an appropriate name for your book. I thought I would never be in this situation, but it can happen to anyone. The Collection Agencies don't leave you alone, and they keep calling, and yes, I keep avoiding them. I want to "Thank You" for your expert advice and for helping many others that are facing this dilemma."

*R.M.C., Tampa, FL*

"This book is amazing. I just wish I had read it before I ran to a bankruptcy lawyer. The collectors were driving my entire family crazy. Now I know how illegal that was."

*Donna W., Albany, NY*

## ACKNOWLEDGMENTS

Special thanks go to Don Gorham, for his wonderful artwork. In addition to being a talented architect and sketch artist, he's a pretty good father-in-law too.

I also thank my editor, Bob Noonan, for his input and revisions.

# CONTENTS

DISCLAIMER

This book provides you with a general overview of the Fair Debt Collection Practices Act (FDCPA), 15 U.S.C. 1692. The FDCPA is a federal law and therefore applicable in all 50 states. However, different circuits and courts interpret law differently. Procedures change, and courts may change their opinions. Always consult an attorney for specific advice. No book can ever replace the sound advice from a lawyer licensed in your own state.

## HOW TO USE THIS BOOK

This book is designed for both lay people and attorneys. Lay people will understand the language and the concepts I have proffered. For attorneys, I have also included a complete bibliography, with footnotes and citations to the law.

This book discusses the Fair Debt Collection Practices Act (FDCPA), 15 U.S.C. 1692 et seq., which is a federal law, and therefore applies to all 50 states. The way the law has been interpreted in different federal jurisdictions, however, may be different than the cases I cited. Courts interpret cases differently from federal jurisdiction to federal jurisdiction. In most instances I have given you the majority rule. Even if your jurisdiction has not issued a ruling on a particular subject, the citations I have given you offer precedent, and tell you how other circuits have decided.

Appendix I contains the complete text of the FDCPA.

Appendix II contains samples of legal complaints for violations of the FDCPA.

Today is Saturday, and the mail just arrived. You received a stack of envelopes, and you'll sort them into two piles: the ones you'll read and the ones you're afraid to read.

The envelopes you *will* open and read are bills you feel you must pay: a credit card you wish to keep current, the car payment, perhaps the utility bill.

The envelopes you *will not* read will sit on your table for a few days, gathering dust. They'll cause you to lose sleep, live in despair, and add to your depression. Even though the envelopes will remain closed, you know they're from debt collectors; they have no names in the return address box to identify the senders, and they all say, "Address Correction Requested" on the lower left-hand corner.

You may look in one envelope to confirm your hunch. Slowly you open it and peek inside, to see the words "Important Notice!" in bold print.

Just last week a debt collector told you that you must not be very responsible if you can't pay your bills. That made you feel terrible about yourself, and lately you've been screening your calls, too, afraid to answer your phone.

As you sink into the couch, you begin to wonder how you ever got into this mess of unpaid bills. A few months ago your credit report was nearly perfect, and you had a steady income. All that has changed. Maybe your spouse left you and the divorce is being finalized; maybe you were laid off; maybe you were hit with a devastating illness. Whatever the reason for your despair, the debt collectors hounding you are adding to your misery.

This book is written for you. This book will teach you how to regain control of your life, and fight back against the debt collector. In addition to helping you get your pride back, this book will make you *want* to open those envelopes, and analyze each and every letter sent you. You'll compare the letters and phone calls you receive from debt collectors with the advice in this book. You'll learn to *take the offensive* against the debt collector.

In fact, perhaps his conduct will even give rise to a lawsuit against him. Did you know that a debt collector can be sued if he makes any misrepresentation, or is insulting, in any of his communications with you? These abuses are so common they're the norm. You have more power than you realize. Even technical violations of the law are enough to trigger your right to sue a collection agency for money damages, costs, and attorney fees.

This book is going to teach you, step by step, how to regain your life. You can sue the debt collector for money damages, and even have them pay for your attorney, for any number of violations. Some are obvious, some are not, but you will learn them. And you will be in control.

An important step in regaining control is restoring your feeling of self worth.

First, realize that *you are not alone*. You are not the only person receiving calls and letters from debt collectors. You are not the only person afraid to open their mail or answer their phone. You are not the only person who has ever lost their job, their spouse, or their health, and found themselves hopelessly in debt over their heads. Let's face it: not having enough money to pay bills is a terrible feeling. It leads to depression, despair, and even marital problems.

Hundreds of years ago, people who owed money—debtors—were actually thrown in jail for not paying their bills. Thank goodness times have changed! While the threat of jail is no longer available to the debt collector, he still knows exactly how to make you feel rotten about yourself. Always remember, you are not alone. The debt collector who just called you is calling hundreds of other people today.

In fact, most of the larger collection agencies have computerized telephone systems. The computer automatically dials one phone number after the next. Your neighbors, your family members, your childrens' teachers are being called. When the collector's automated dialing system dials your number, your account information automatically pops up on the collector's screen. After your phone call, the collector will type a few notations under your account information, and the computer will dial the next person's number.

You are nothing but a number to the debt collector.

We all know about failed dot.coms, airlines, and retailers. Businesses face more financial problems than individuals do. Yet businesses never feel the same pangs of guilt and fear that consumers feel when being chased by a debt collector. Consumers run from answering their phones and opening their letters; businesses have power lunches and meetings in their think-tank offices, trying to develop strategies for keeping the wolf away from the door. Businesses take a *less personal* approach to financial ruin.

Consumers, however, take debt very personally. Debt collectors prey on your weakness. Making people feel bad about themselves is a powerful collection tool.

It's also illegal.

As an attorney, I have spent the last decade suing collection agencies, car dealers, and credit reporting agencies for violations of consumer protection laws. I'm also a bankruptcy attorney. One of my trademarks is that I make house calls. People love having their lawyer come to their home. They're more comfortable discussing intimate problems such as finances in their own living room, rather than the sterilized atmosphere of an attorney's office.

When we're sitting down at their table, the time for the big question has arrived. "How much debt do you have?" I ask.

People will always avoid eye contact as they push the large pile of bills across the table towards me. Invariably, most of the envelopes are unopened. These people have been beaten and battered by debt collectors so much, they're afraid to open their mail.

My clients marvel when I tell them I have done many bankruptcies for many of their neighbors. I do not identify them, of course; I just want my new clients to know that many of their neighbors are sharing the same feelings of desperation that they are.

I also point out all the wealthy people who have been in financial ruin. Many celebrities have filed for bankruptcy. You can be an actor, a doctor, a CEO; all of us, often for completely unexpected reasons, can be a step away from homelessness.

*All* of us, at one time or another, have received phone calls and letters from debt collectors. Debt collection transcends class lines, and affects every socioeconomic class.

I know this only too well. It happened to me.

# CHAPTER 1

# MY STORY

**M**any years ago, the delinquency rate in the loan department of a very large financial institution was sky-high, and a good chance existed that the banking authorities would come in and close the place down. So, one year out of law school, I was hired on a consulting basis to bring the institution's delinquency under control.

My background had nothing to do with debt collection. My father, in fact, was an accident investigator and testified at trials as to injuries and liability. I had worked at his side since I was a boy, and investigations were all I knew. In law school I expanded my horizons, and took a job as a clerk with a firm that specialized in bankruptcy. I worked on a variety of bankruptcy cases, from large corporations to individuals.

Then, while studying for the bar exam, I worked in the collection department of a bank. There I saw the opposite end of the bankruptcy business; suddenly I was playing the role of debt collector as opposed to bankruptcy lawyer. It was quickly obvious that these two positions were at odds with one another.

The bank had an automated dialing system, a device I had never heard of before. We collectors sat in front of computer monitors, and a computer would automatically dial numbers. Suddenly, a person's account information would pop up on the screen: name, address, phone number, account number, balance, payment history.

When someone answered the phone I would ask who I was talking to, and then introduce myself and ask for the account holder. More often than not, I would get hung up on. Others were polite. Still others screamed at me and told me not to call again. I was earning approximately $8 an hour, big bucks back in the late 80s for a law student with $70,000 in student loans.

In between calls I would sit there and listen to other collectors. There was one fellow, who I'll call Jim, who would scream and swear loudly into the phone at the bank's delinquent customers. Jim would then turn around in his swivel chair with his arms folded, and look at everyone to make sure we all heard him. The manager would come over to hear the commotion, and Jim would tell her what an idiot that particular consumer was. Some people would chuckle. Jim elevated himself to hero status on the grounds that he was meaner than everyone else.

(For the rest of this book I will refer to all debt collectors as "he." This is not because all debt collectors are male; rather, it's because most of the truly mean debt collectors I've encountered are men. I've spoken to stern female debt collectors, but I have never sued because of something a female debt collector said or did.)

Back to the bank. Hanging on the wall behind us was a bar chart, with all our names on it. Every week the manager would take a red magic marker and graph out how much money each person had collected that week. The person who collected the most at the end of the month would get a prize: a dress down day, a day off, maybe a few movie tickets.

As for my own debt collection style, I was friendly and pleasant. I would talk to the person and explain that I knew things were tough, but say that if they could send me *something* I would be happy.

I never won the prize with my soft-styled approach, but I always came in second or third. Where did Jim place? Several positions below me. His meanness accomplished nothing, except to make people—myself included—hate him and everything he stood for.

Working for my large corporate client, I had the opportunity to meet with many debt collection lawyers. I was given tours of their office, met their staff, saw the computerized systems that churned out lawsuits and letters faster than even the best legal secretary. And I was frequently taken out to lunch at the finest restaurants in Manhattan. I've seen the bill for four people come to $300, with an additional $100 tip left. These collectors were high rollers.

There I was, a country boy turned big-city debt collector, with a private practice on the side. Life was good. I was sitting on top of the world.

I used my investigative background to find people, and discover where they were hiding assets. My bankruptcy experience gave me working knowledge of how to treat files that were in bankruptcy. My rapidly increasing collection experience added to the mix. The delinquency rate in my department plummeted. I received great performance reviews. I wasn't a good debt collector; I was a *great* debt collector.

We've all heard the saying, "What goes up, must come down." Ten years ago, at the peak of my career, I was sitting in my office when my phone rang. It was my father. He was having a heart attack.

As I drove that evening to the hospital 150 miles away, I started reflecting on the way my life was going. I was a country boy, and appreciated nature and an easy life. Now I was working seven days a week, 12 hours a day, and spending money as fast as I was making it. The call I received from my father put the brakes on my life: He was dying, and I was too busy to spend some time with him?

My father's illness was just the first in a series of setbacks. My wife also became seriously ill. I found myself unable to function. My thoughts could not focus; I would stare at piles of paper for an entire afternoon, and actually had to hire someone to help me do the work.

Finally I gave notice to my job, told my wife we would get by on what I'd make as a solo practitioner in my country town, packed my belongings, and drove off into the sunset on a cold Friday evening.

I spent the next several weeks visiting my father at home and in the hospital. I had no money coming in, but could not even attempt to generate new income with my thoughts and emotions so scrambled. My savings were soon eaten up by bills, and the polite letters from debt collectors started coming. "You appear to have missed a payment." Before I knew it, meaner letters were arriving. Then the phone would ring. "When can we expect payment?" I assured them it would be soon, and explained what I was going through. But they didn't care. They wanted the money, now.

I spoke to collection managers, told them I was a lawyer, and assured them they would all get paid. I just needed time to get my life back in order. They didn't care. They wanted the money, now.

I tried to barter my services. I offered to collect for them, and let them keep my fee as bill payment. They weren't interested.

Then my father died. Just a few weeks later, a process server served me a summons on a bill. I called the lawyer who was suing me and begged him for the professional courtesy of allowing me an extension to answer the lawsuit. I was, after all, one of them.

He didn't care.

Because I had the same name as my father, the collectors began calling my father's home, distressing my mother. The calls got worse; "What kind of lawyer are you, anyway?" one collector shouted. The mail and stacks of unpaid bills began to pile up. I was afraid to answer the phone or go to my mailbox.

I wasn't a bad person. I was a good person who had fallen from economic stability because of circumstances beyond my control. I just wanted these people to listen to me! But in their eyes I was no longer a New York City attorney with a big income and successful career. I was now nothing more than a debtor, a deadbeat.

I realized I had become the very same type of person whose life I had previously been making miserable, and I was suddenly ashamed of myself.

At that point I knew that if I didn't fight back, I'd be overwhelmed. I knew a particular federal law governed debt collectors; in fact I was actually pretty well versed in what that law said. But I needed particulars. I needed to know who had been sued in the past, and why, and who had won.

I got a copy of the law, the *Fair Debt Collection Practices Act,* and studied it and the cases that interpreted it. I read what the courts were saying about debt collectors. I discovered they *could* be sued successfully. One jury had even granted a woman many millions of dollars against a collector who had phoned her a bomb threat!

I realized then and there that I did not have to listen to the screaming, the derogatory tones, the insults. I decided to fight back.

I analyzed the law and the cases until I understood the complexities, but one more problem existed. Would I hire a lawyer, or represent myself? I had never sued anyone. I had studied civil procedure in law school, but had no practical experience.

I took the facts of my first case and called some lawyer friends of mine to see if they'd represent me. I was embarrassed to tell them the jam I was in, but I had to. I described in painstaking detail why I thought the dirty deeds done to me were illegal. The acts were so secretive, there was no way a lay person would have been able to see the trickery and deceit. With my investigative and lawyer skills I had figured out the scam; now, I needed help.

My friends all gave me the same response. "Sounds wrong, but what can we do?" I knew they were simply being honest; none of them represented consumers, none of them knew the law, and none of them had any idea what to do.

I then did what every good American does in time of need: I opened the yellow pages. I started calling lawyers, one by one. I got the same reply from each. Sorry. If the case of *Me v. Them* was to proceed, I was on my own.

I was completely frustrated, but determined not to let these scoundrels get away with their scam. I reviewed my rules on civil procedure, and then I served a Summons and Complaint on my adversary. I took them to court.

What did they do?

The credit industry is very large, very powerful, and very rich. I learned this firsthand when they hired not one, but two large law firms, all to try and beat little me, a solo practitioner working in a small apartment. They filed motion after motion against me, including a motion for sanctions. They wanted the court to punish me with a fine, and payment of their $200 an hour attorney fees.

I called my uncle, himself a highly experienced lawyer, and told him I was terrified because I had just received my first motion for sanctions.

"Are they right?" he asked, meaning, was my lawsuit so frivolous the court should punish me?

"No," I responded, "they're just trying to bully me out of this lawsuit."

"Well," said my uncle, "then you file a motion for sanctions, saying *their* motion for sanctions is sanctionable."

And I did!

The lawsuit became a standing joke between my wife and me. Every Monday we'd wait for the mail to arrive, because Monday was the day I always received my next round of motion papers. The big firms had secretaries, paralegals, associates, computerized research, and law libraries. I, on the other hand, went to the law school and typed my own papers. I was out-numbered and out-financed, and certainly more than a bit intimidated about the size of my opponents. I had to always ask myself: Am I right? In my heart I knew I was, and that drove me to continue the fight.

I also learned something incredibly important about this industry: When you sue a debt collector the industry fights to the end, because every failure sets precedent against other debt collectors. If a collector loses a case in one court, that decision will be available on computer and easily accessible to virtually everyone. The credit industry treats every single case as a potential threat to its livelihood, and to the way it makes money off the backs of the working poor and middle class. After all, one ruling against them in a court of law could have ramifications throughout the entire country. They're afraid of the message sent out. They'll always appeal a decision against them, to try and tire their adversary. The industry protects itself. They actively discuss cases they have won and lost, and they monitor the tactics they can use against you.

What was the end result of *Me v. Them?* The case was settled out of court, in my favor. The industry did not want an adverse decision, so they paid me money to make me go away. The fact that they settled proved I could fight back and win. I learned an awful lot about litigating these matters during that period of my life.

But something else even more important happened: The credit industry created an enemy, a consumer advocate.

Since that time I have been representing consumers in court, against the credit industry. I also give seminars to people from all walks of life, and I've taught Continuing Legal Education credits on consumer advocacy to lawyers. I'm proud of who I am, and the very difficult lessons I learned back then.

In this book I'm sharing my knowledge with you. I'm sharing the tricks and scams I have uncovered. I'm telling you the law, to save you the hundreds of hours it took me to figure it all out. I'm teaching you to fight back and win. I'm drawing on my years of experience as an investigator, a bankruptcy lawyer, a debt collector, and my own experience as a man whose soul was tormented by acts beyond his control.

You are not alone. I am with you. You will be able to control the debt collector if you just follow the advice in this book. I have even cited specific cases, with which to sharpen your own axe.

Read on. Stand tall. *You* are in control.

# THE FAIR DEBT COLLECTION PRACTICES ACT

The tools I'm going to give you in this book are based on the Fair Debt Collection Practices Act (FDCPA), a federal law written specifically to protect you, the consumer, from unfair and deceptive debt collection practices. It is the legal basis of your right and ability to protect yourself, and it will be referred to throughout this book. The entire law is quoted in Appendix I, and I ask you to refer to it every time I cite a proposition. The FDCPA prohibits *only* deceptive and unfair acts and practices in an attempt to collect a debt incurred for personal, family, or household purposes. The key to the FDCPA is the tricks the collection agency uses, and how the courts interpret the legality of those tricks.

Want to know how commonplace illegal collection techniques are? Consider this opening statement from the FDCPA:

### Section 1692 (a) Abusive practices.

"There is abundant evidence of the use of abusive, deceptive, and unfair debt collection practices by many debt collectors. Abusive debt collection practices contribute to the number of personal bankruptcies, to marital instability, to the loss of jobs, and to invasions of personal privacy."

We'll get into more detail about specific illegal activities later, but here's an example of one.

A collector told a woman, "You shouldn't be having children if you can't afford to pay for their hospital bills."

This is a completely illegal statement. Even though debt collectors thrive on making you feel terrible about yourself, often what they say and write to you, and the actions they threaten to take, are completely illegal. If collectors make illegal statements, or try to humiliate you, or threaten legal action they cannot legally take, *you have the right to actually sue them and get money damages—perhaps even enough money to pay your debt off.*

How much can you sue them for? The FDCPA allows punitive damages of $1,000, costs and attorney fees, and "actual damages."

Most lawyers see that $1,000 figure and run from a debt collection case, thinking it isn't worth the time for so little money. Even the lawyers representing the debt collectors start negotiations with, "You can only get $1,000." But this is *wrong.* They fail to take a closer look at the "actual damages" clause. This includes *emotional distress damage,* and on these, the sky is the limit. Since most debt collectors work hard to make you feel bad about yourself, as a collection tool, this clause very often applies.

Don't forget you're also entitled to costs and attorney fees; 100% of them, if the court so orders. That means your attorney can collect on every billable hour of work he puts into your case.

A variety of state and common laws also apply, and, depending on the particular law, substantial punitive damages can be awarded. Massachusetts, for example, has a law called 93A, which allows for *triple damages.* These laws are called UDAP laws, meaning Unlawful Deceptive Acts and Practices. Ask your lawyer to research what consumer protection laws your state has. This book does not address state UDAP laws; we only discuss the national law.

You can also sue on a wide variety of other claims, including but not limited to: intentional infliction of emotional distress; fraud and misrepresentation; civil conspiracy; negligence; and perhaps even racketeering.

How many debt collectors use illegal collection techniques? In my opinion, for every one honest debt collector, there are two crooked ones. If all the people in America stopped paying their bills tomorrow, within a few short months at *least* 50% of them could file lawsuits for illegal debt collection practices.

The FDCPA is a bland statute, and if you read it, you'll probably shrug your shoulders and say to yourself, "What's the big deal?" Many debt collectors say the same thing. That attitude leads them to violate the law, providing you with the rights to take them to court, and get money damages for their violations.

Lawyers have to take Continuing Legal Education (CLE) courses every year, in order to keep their law licenses. CLE courses vary from state to state, but usually fall into the usual categories of trusts and estates, personal injury, and even bankruptcy. I was given the honor of teaching one of my county's first seminars on consumer protection for CLE credit. Consumer protection is not taught in law schools, therefore few law practitioners concentrate in it, so it's extremely difficult to find a CLE course on the subject. Ironically, most consumer protection classes in the past have been taught by—you guessed it—debt collection attorneys! These attorneys will conveniently not mention FDCPA violations that may launch class action suits against them, and will almost always routinely mention and dwell on obvious but useless facts like, "Debt collectors can't call you at 3 a.m."

Upon closer inspection, however, the FDCPA proves to be one of the most thrilling areas of law. The FDCPA has been interpreted by courts in a very *pro-consumer* manner. The collection industry has a never-ending pool of schemes to use on consumers, each one trickier than the next, and many of them violate the FDCPA. Sadly, however, only a relative few lawyers are what you could call true consumer protection attorneys. With the glut of lawyers in this country, only a handful are dedicated to combating the crimes committed against consumers by the credit industry. Perhaps more lawyers will dedicate their practices to consumer protection when they discover that what appears as a "bland" law actually requires a fascinating look into the fraud routinely perpetrated by the credit industry.

This book comes complete with actual case citations for the law I'm teaching you. If you have encountered a debt collection violation, you'll be able to take this book to your attorney and show him the law that has been violated. Just do yourself one favor: Make sure your lawyer does not represent banks, and does not collect debts.

One more point: The FDCPA applies only to *consumer* debt. This is debt obtained for personal, family or household purposes. It can include, but is not limited to, credit card debt, medical bills, student loans, repossessions, and, at least in New York, and under certain circumstances, even eviction proceedings. The FDCPA does not apply to commercial debt, such as business loans.

# CHAPTER 3

# START A JOURNAL

To successfully sue debt collectors, you must have accurate documentation of their communication with you. So now you must start a journal. We want to place you in the strategic position of keeping track of *every* letter you receive from *every* debt collector, and the contents of *every* phone conversation you have with him. This journal will assist us in determining whether any laws have been broken.

As you will see later in the book, a debt collector does not have to make extraordinarily nasty statements to break the debt collection laws. Often a simple letter can trigger an FDCPA violation, even if it is quite innocent sounding.

You must save all the collections letters you receive. I also want you to open them now, and place them before you. I know it hurts to look at them, but we must analyze them within the confines of the FDCPA. If you can imagine yourself as merely a number, and one of thousands who received a collection letter, you won't take the attacks as personal. In fact, the collector sending you the letter may even be in the same debt situation you are.

Pay careful attention to *writing down* details about phone conversations you have with the collector. Whereas we have a written record of the communication with the letters, no such record exists with telephone conversations. Telephone records always disappear. If we determine that a collection agency has violated the FDCPA, you and your lawyer will have to prove your case. In order to prove your case, you must have *specific facts* regarding phone communications you had with the collector: his name (even a desk name), date of call, time of call, and content of communication. You should also keep copies of all communications sent to the collector, and his responses to you.

The journal must contain the following information:

1. the name, address and date the letter was received;
2. written records of every phone call received from every debt collector, stating:
   a. date of the call;
   b. name, address, and phone number of the debt collector;
   c. who he's collecting for; and
   d. sum and substance of the conversation.

To avoid a "he said, she said" scenario, write down as much of the conversation as possible.

Want the collector to hang up fast? Ask him if you can tape record the conversation for "quality control" purposes! They can do it; why can't we?

Now you've taken control, and have started accumulating evidence that will help you. And now you must learn who your adversary is! Their names, who they work for, and their location. They know all this information about you; now you must learn it about them.

# CHAPTER 4

# WHO IS THIS DEBT COLLECTOR?

He knows who you are; he has all your vital and personal financial information downloaded on his computer. You, however, know nothing about him. You probably don't even know his real name, because many debt collectors use fake names, called "desk names" in the industry.

The collector on the phone with you is just one cog in a multi-billion dollar industry. He has attended seminars and had training and experience in how to make you pay, what to say to you, and how to ruin your credit. The collector belongs to several professional collector groups, and has attended professional conventions. At these conventions, industry representatives discuss tactics and techniques for collecting money that work and don't work. Tricks of the trade. Scams.

The representatives attend these conventions with lawyers who represent them against lawsuits brought by consumer protection attorneys, such as myself. The industry lawyers discuss how to quash other lawyers who have attempted to fight their various schemes.

Some businesses even run collector "camps." The debt collector gathers up his hard-to-collect accounts, and off to camp he goes. There he will learn not only what to say, but what tone of voice to use on the phone with you; when he should be angry, and when he should talk nicely. These camps help him hone his skills and techniques.

You alone, without the advice from this book, are no match for the professional debt collector. He has studied at length how to get into your psyche and control you. You, on the other hand, have probably just suffered a crisis in your life, such as a loss of a marriage, a job, or health, and are wallowing in despair. The debt collector knows you are probably suffering from self-pity, and has been taught a variety of strategies to manipulate those feelings, and make you talk.

If you have any doubt whatsoever as to the strength of the credit/collection industry, consider this. As this very chapter is being written, the credit industry has been buying Congress with huge donations, to change the bankruptcy laws. Bankruptcy is the last bastion of hope for millions of Americans buried in debt. The industry that helped put them there is now buying your Congressman with large sums of money, to further close bankruptcy doors, so you have no way out.

A person standing alone is no match for someone so trained, with so much money behind them. This is accepted as so obvious that the law itself regards the average person as "the least sophisticated consumer." The "least sophisticated consumer" label applies to anyone, regardless of their education. The assumption by the courts is that the consumer knows nothing, and is no match for the industry.

Collectors come from all walks of life. The career collectors are usually the agency owners and attorneys who specialize in debt collection. Their employees, the foot soldiers of the industry, are the representatives you'll have contact with. These foot soldiers get paid decently, anywhere from minimum wage to maybe $10-$12 an hour. Collectors who work for large agencies often work on a commission basis. They receive, in addition to an hourly fee, a percentage of what they collect. Annual incomes for commission-based collectors can reach six figures! Management, certainly, gets paid more.

The foot soldiers—the collectors who do the calling—usually respond to a newspaper ad for a job as a collector. No special training is required, except the ability to make people pay, and be heartless. The usual "training tool" for the new collector is a manual of computer codes, and a copy of the FDCPA, the law we will be examining. The collector is told to read the FDCPA, but is rarely provided more education about this very important law. Agencies spend more time teaching their collectors how to *break* the law, than to follow it. Greed is everywhere in the industry.

The collector trainee will usually listen in on other collectors' calls on a headset during their conversation, to hear how his trainer handles different calls. You'll never know if a trainee is listening in on your conversation. And the supervisors—who know all the tricks and scams—are never more than a few offices away.

The job starts out as one of last resort for many people, because of the low skill required. They most likely lost their job just like you, and are looking for something temporary until a better job is found. Once they realize the work is not hard and the pay is pretty good, they decide to stick around a while.

Collection agencies themselves vary greatly. Some agencies are very large, and collect millions of dollars. Others are very small, and may actually consist of one person working out of their garage. Anyone with a laptop computer and the right software can call themselves a collector. You can buy the software on the open market, and can print official-looking telegrams and letterhead. After you have the software, you can go door-to-door to doctors' offices and small businesses, and market yourself as a collector.

Many agencies offer perks and incentives to their collectors. The perk can be simple: If a collector brings in more money than his colleagues do in a given month, he gets a day off, or a movie ticket.

All debt collectors have monthly quotas. Your collector will frequently tell you that he needs your payment by the end of the week, and will often insist that you send the check by overnight mail. This false impression of urgency is usually put on you just so the collector can meet his quota.

## COLLECTORS USE DESK NAMES

The collector calling you is probably not giving you his real name. Many debt collectors use "desk names," so people won't know their true identity. They say they do this to protect themselves, so people won't be able to hunt them down or stalk them. I say it is just the first act of deception you'll face.

Even the computers that issue collection letters to you have desk names. If a large agency sends out letters, and the letter is signed, for example, by "C. Bass," that could be the name of the computer. When you call the agency and ask to speak with C. Bass, the switchboard operator knows you're calling because you received a collection letter, and will automatically forward your call to the collection department.

These desk names can also indicate categories of delinquency. If you're 30 days late—barely delinquent—the letter may be signed, for example, "Brooke Trout." When you call asking to speak to Brooke, the call is sent to the department that handles 30-day accounts. "C. Bass" may be reserved for accounts that are 60 or 90 days late.

The use of desk names is, for the most part, legal.

## THE "POWER OVER" PLOY

Whether the collector works for a large or small agency, one theme runs consistently through the collection industry: *The collector wants you to think he has power over you.* The strategy is to make you feel you owe the collector something. I don't care if the collector is nice to you or not, he or she will try, directly or indirectly, to achieve power over you.

Achieving that "power over" status is extremely simple. You owe money you don't have, therefore you're inferior. If you just went through a divorce or lost your job, you probably feel terrible about yourself already. The debt collector doesn't have to do much coaxing to make you feel completely helpless against him. A variety of strategies may be used.

## GOOD GUY-BAD GUY

The collector may be nice to you, or mean. Collectors often employ the "good guy-bad guy" strategy: The nice collector will be friendly and understanding, but allude, "You had better deal with me, otherwise I will have no choice but to transfer the account to another, meaner collector."

The "good guy-bad guy" psychology is extremely effective. A debt collector, as you will see, is highly limited in what he can do. This is why psychological tactics to make you feel inferior are so important to them.

Why would a bank, which has fewer legal restrictions on their collection methods than a collection agency, transfer the account to someone who has less power to collect a debt? Again, psychology. Simply receiving a letter from a third party is enough to prompt a majority of people into paying. The psychology is, "The account was transferred to the bad guy. They mean business. I'd better pay." That's why some law firms will even send out an initial "dunn" letter for a $10 fee, without actually having the account assigned to them for collection.

The "nice" collector may actually pretend to care about your problems. When the collector asks you why you didn't pay a bill, your typical response might be, "I lost my job." The conversation will then turn to where you worked, what you did, are you looking for new work, are you paying your other bills, does your spouse work, do you own a home, and so forth. All this information is gleaned from you under the impression you have a sympathetic ear. But in actuality the debt collector is simply collecting information about you, for collection purposes. For example, if they ask, "Are you looking for another job?" you might ramble on about your job in the local supermarket. You unfortunately just told the collector where you work, so they know where to garnish your wages if collection activities "ripen" to a judgment.

Keep this clearly in mind: *The collector is not, and never will be, your friend.* I discuss in later chapters what the collector may say to you, but take one lesson with you now: *Tell the collector nothing.* They do not care about you, and any question they ask should be *ignored.* You may owe a bill, but you owe the collector nothing—not even respect. *Don't forget that.*

Still another scenario is, "If you don't pay I'll have to transfer your account to another department."

## TALKING DOWN TO YOU

Another collector's tactic is to call you by your first name, and refer to themselves as "Mr." or "Ms." For example, "Hello, Susan, this is Mr. Bigelow calling." Calling you by your first name and expecting you to call them "Mr." is another "power over" ploy. You're made to think, and feel, that you're talking to a superior.

If you get one of these calls, tell the collector that you can either both speak to each other by first names, or by Ms. or Mr., but you refuse to call him Mr. if he doesn't reciprocate.

Being professional and firm, but courteous and polite, will tell this person from your very first communication that he cannot take advantage of you.

The collector may also say, "You didn't call me back when I called the other day," or, "I told you to call me back."

Excuse me? A complete stranger is calling you in the privacy of your home, demanding to know why you didn't call him back?

You do *not* owe the collector a call back—ever.

If you step back from the stress you're under and analyze the situation, you'll see how in control you actually are!

You owe this collector *nothing*. You don't owe him a call back. You don't owe him explanations as to why the debt is unpaid. You don't owe him any promises. In fact, as you will see in the following chapters, you don't even owe him one shred of courtesy.

The collector owes *you*. You have the money he wants.

The laws we will examine state that he owes you respect. No law anywhere, and I mean anywhere—except under order from a court of law, or a subpoena—states you owe him answers, explanations, or, for that matter, says you even have to accept his phone calls.

Do *not* tell the debt collector where you work, how much you make, the name of your bank, what your spouse does, or any other personal information. The collector is not even telling you his real name, why should you tell him anything about yourself?

## DEMANDING MONEY IMMEDIATELY

Another example of the concept of "power over" is the statement, "I need the check by this Friday."

Collectors love demanding payment by a certain day, and then state, "My client says that if they don't have the check by Friday they will sue you."

If the check arrives Monday, will the "client" really still sue you? Of course they won't. The stated deadline is just another way to have power over you. When the collector states the check must be received by a certain date, you find yourself scrambling to overnight deliver a check, hoping it doesn't bounce until next payday. Once again, you're on the defensive, and you're not in control.

I'd like to make two points in this regard.

First, if the agent insists on overnight delivery, make *them* pay for it. You shouldn't have to pay for overnight mail. All of these agencies have an overnight account, and will hand the account number over when pressed. So press them.

Practically, it should make no difference if a check arrives a day or two later by regular U.S. mail. The debt collector will always make up a scheme as to why overnight is necessary.

Once in a while, a creditor will "draw a line in the sand" and demand that a check must be received by a certain day, for example, when making a settlement offer. But if that line has not been drawn, no reason exists for you to have to overnight the check. The debt collector has absolutely no right to demand it, and you have every right to say no. You have the money in your hands. He wants your money. Send it the way you want. If the debt collector gets rude with you, don't listen to him. Hang up if you want. You do not have to do what he requests.

The second point is this: the collector may make a settlement offer. He may say something like, "If I get this check by Friday, I'll settle the entire account for 40% of the balance due." If you're made an offer similar to this one, send that check in, and overnight it! When faced with an offer of settlement, it is appropriate to overnight the check. Receiving the check is a condition precedent to the contract to settle.

Make sure the check gets there, though. I've seen consumers reach an agreement with an agency for 40% of the balance, and the check didn't arrive at the agency by the agreed deadline. The collector received the check one day later, which lets them out of the agreement. They then proceed to collect more from you, under the guise that you did not meet the deadline.

# CHAPTER 5

# WHAT IS A "COLLECTION AGENCY?"

**W**hat company the collector is calling you *from* is important, because it determines which rights you have under the law. Not all laws apply to all categories of debt collectors. We're focusing our analysis on the Fair Debt Collection Practices Act (FDCPA).

Collectors generally fall into two categories, depending on their employers. The first category is in-house collectors. These are employees of the businesses that you actually borrowed the money from: banks, credit companies, credit unions, and credit card companies. These collectors tell you they're calling from their business, and the letters they send you are on their business' letterhead. The FDCPA does not apply to collectors who work for the people who extended credit to you.

Chapter 14 tells you how to deal with in-house collectors. Even though the FDCPA does not apply to in-house collectors, you should still follow the analysis in this book. In-house collections often still follow the FDCPA as a guideline. They just can't be sued for violating the FDCPA.

On the other hand, the second category, third-party collectors, *must* comply with the FDCPA. Third-party collectors can be broken down into five categories:

1. collection agencies;
2. law firms that derive a majority of their income from collections;
3. "pretend" third-party collectors (actually working for creditors);
4. skip-tracers; and
5. purchaser's of debt.

Although the FDCPA applies to third-party collectors, banks and creditors had themselves completely excluded from the FDCPA. If you doubted the power of the credit industry, all doubt should be removed by now. In 1978, banks had the one federal law designed to protect consumers from collectors not apply to their own collectors. This is unfair.

The reasoning behind the Congressional decision was this: A consumer has a choice of what banks to go to, but does not have a choice what collection agency the bank turns his delinquent account over to. If the consumer is dissatisfied with the way the bank collects its debt, so the logic went, the consumer could just change banks. However, a consumer cannot change the collection agency that the bank referred the account to for collection.

Obviously this reasoning was ludicrous, and if it was ludicrous back then it certainly is now. Today hundreds of banks have merged, narrowing consumer choice drastically. Except for a few remaining hometown banks, the industry is overcome with conglomerates. While the push by Congress to restrict bankruptcy is on, I do not see on the horizon, any time soon, any reform expanding the FDCPA to apply to banks.

When a creditor—one who extends credit, such as a bank or credit card company—is unable to collect on a loan, they have several options concerning what to do with the delinquent loan. The creditor may write the loan off and take it as a loss. They may sell the loan, for pennies on the dollar, to companies that specialize in buying bad debt, which they then try to collect for themselves. Or the creditor may transfer the bad debt to a third-party collection agency (or to a law firm specializing in collections).

When the creditor decides to hire a debt collector to try and collect the loan, your loan information is transferred to the collector. This information includes your loan application, payment history, checking account information, credit reports, and any notations on your account, such as previous collection attempts.

The term "collection agency," as used in this book, refers to a third-party business, *unrelated* to the original creditor, that is collecting a debt. The term "collection agency" also refers to a business that purchased the original debt, and is in the business of collecting the purchased debt in its *own* name.

A law firm may or may not be a debt collector. To be a debt collector, the law firm must collect delinquent debts as a regular part of its business. If it's a personal injury firm, and does one collection account a year, it's arguably not a debt collector, and the FDCPA will not apply. Many law firms, however, do collect on accounts on a regular basis, and their actions fall under FDCPA jurisdiction.

The term "pretend third-party agency" means a creditor that has established a department within its own organization, which department collects debts, and has a name different than the main business. The purpose is to give the impression that the account was turned over to a third party.

The term "skip-tracer" refers to a person or separate entity which specializes in locating people or assets for the purpose of debt collection.

The FDCPA also applies to purchasers' of debt. A purchaser is an agency that buys blocks of debt for pennies on the dollar, and then tries to collect on them. Many large banks and finance companies sell "problem debt," that is, delinquent accounts. The bank simply does not want to be bothered with the collection of these accounts. Furthermore, there may be some very real, legitimate reasons why the account has not paid.

Purchasers buy blocks of debt for very low prices. For example, they may pay as little as $5,000 for as much as $250,000 in debt! If the purchaser collects on every account, it made $245,000 on an initial investment of $5,000! How's that for a return on investment!?

# CHAPTER 6

# HOW DID THE COLLECTOR FIND YOU?

A special group of debt collectors called "skip-tracers" are in the business of finding consumers. The consumer "skipped" town, hence the name skip-tracer.

Usually, the skip-tracer does not actually call you trying to collect money. Instead, a debt collection agency will hire a skip-tracer to *find* you. Some of the larger debt collection agencies actually have their own department of skip-tracers. In addition to locating people, skip-tracers also specialize in finding assets, once the collection account has been reduced to a judgment.

When a debt collector receives your account in his office, his first concern is to locate you. The collector needs an address to send letters to, and a phone number to call you with.

If you moved away from your old residence convinced no one could locate you, and suddenly the debt collector is on the phone asking for money, you were "skipped" and didn't even realize it. How were you found? Skip-tracers are a dubious group. They too must follow the FDCPA. However, their violations may be so secretive you'll never know they broke the law, until you analyze how they found you or confirmed your address and phone number.

## HOW DOES A SKIP-TRACER LOCATE YOU?

Skip-tracers employ a variety of both legal and illegal ways to find someone. More unscrupulous skip-tracers apply a variety of highly unethical techniques.

The first step a skip-tracer will take is to look at your loan application. Often the application asks for information such as nearest relative, residences in the last five years, bank account information, and the name of a person to call in case of an emergency. The application even requests your mother's maiden name.

While this information may provide useful steps to determine initial credit worthiness, it also provides a lot of information to *find* you, should you ever move and not leave a forwarding address. The personal information requested benefits you very little; the true benefit is to the creditor. He has just obtained information that will assist in collecting this debt, should you ever default on your repayment obligation.

When we fill out a loan application, the application always asks for your mother's or wife's maiden name. You probably thought this was for security purposes. You thought wrong. Actually, the information provides the debt collector with the rest of your family tree to call and prompt for information about you.

What a skip-tracer is allowed to do is found in the FDCPA, Section 1692b (Appendix I).

The skip tracer can legally:

1. identify himself;
2. state he is confirming your location; and
3. identify his employer (if requested).

The skip-tracer cannot:

1. tell anyone you owe a debt;
2. call the same person more than once, unless he believes the first response as to where you were was incomplete;
3. communicate by postcard;
4. use an envelope with a return address indicating the name of a collection agency; and
5. talk to anyone after the debt collector knows you have an attorney.

The skip-tracer will first scan your loan or credit application for valuable information. He can then legally call your relatives, to see if they've heard from you. He may start with the name listed under "Whom to call in case of an emergency."

The collector also has your mother's maiden name. If you got married or changed your name, the skip-tracer can find your relatives by doing searches under your mother's maiden name.

The skip-tracer also can conduct what is known as a "nearby." Books exist which provide every single address in a city, who lives at that address, and what the phone number there is. If you have caller ID and repeatedly refuse to answer the phone, the skip-tracer can call a neighbor and ask them to give you a message. This is legal, as long as they comply with Section 1692b of the FDCPA.

The skip-tracer can also call your old neighbors, and ask them if they know where you moved to. Usually the skip-tracer will say he's a friend who lost contact with you. If he says this, he misrepresented himself. He lied. You can sue him under the FDCPA.

The loan application also has banking information on it. The skip-tracer can call the bank listed on the application and inquire if the account is still open. If it is, the bank will have the address where it is sending your statements, and will share that information with the skip-tracer.

The skip-tracer may also order your credit report. Every time you apply for credit, your latest address appears on the top of the credit report requested by the lending institution.

A client of mine had moved to a new address to hide from creditors. He called a bottling company to have water delivered to his new address, and the customer service rep asked him several questions. She also pulled a credit report on him. In the process of pulling the report, she entered his new address and the other information into the computer. What followed was a barrage of letters from the debt collectors my client had been avoiding.

The skip-tracer will also send a letter to your last known address, to determine if you still live there. You can tell if you've received one of these letters without even opening it up, because it will say "Address Correction Requested" on it.

Why write "Address Correction Requested" on an envelope? Because if you've moved and left a forwarding address, and "Address Correction Requested" is on the envelope, the post office will place your *new* address on a yellow sticker, and send the new address back to the sender. And the skip-tracer has found you. If "Address Correction Requested" is not on the envelope, the envelope will automatically be forwarded to you, and the skip-tracer won't know where it went. The words "Address Correction Requested" are the trigger that sends your new address back to the sender.

If the skip-tracer has pulled your credit report, he will also call each and every other creditor you have, and ask them if they know where you are. This is particularly useful to the skip-tracer if you are paying some bills but not others. The collector can then obtain information regarding your new address, bank information, and even employment information.

Each creditor on your credit report has a code identification number. The skip-tracer will cross-reference the code number with a chart of codes, and get the phone number and address for the creditor he wants to call. He will start the conversation by saying, "Hi, my name is John, and I am trying to do a skip on Jane Doe." The employee of the creditor will then pull your account up and tell the skip-tracer what address he has for you, and what information he has on the bank you are paying your bills from.

The bank is another source of information about you. Every time you send a check to someone to pay a bill, the receiver of the check writes down the name and address of your bank, and the account number. Even though your check was cashed and sent back to you with the monthly statement, a full record of the check is maintained by the creditor.

Other sources of information about you include motor vehicle records and voter registration information. A simple check at the state Department of Motor Vehicles will provide an address, and even limited asset information.

The Internet has made this practice even more sophisticated than it was just a few years ago.

## CALLER ID

The pen register, or "trap device," as it is called, has moved out of the hands of law enforcement and into everyone's household. Pen register is the technical name for caller ID. Widespread use of the pen register has provided a trap for the unwary.

There is no right to privacy in a phone number. The use of caller ID to trace people is legal. How this number is obtained may be subject to regulation, however.[1]

## HOW TO READ AN ENVELOPE

Learn how to read an envelope. If I send you a letter, and I don't want you to know it's from me, a simple return address such as "Rich, 12065-0104" is sufficient. When the "least sophisticated consumer" sees an address of "Rich, 12065-0104" they become very confused. "Rich" may be a desk name. The consumer also has no idea where the envelope came from.

But it's easy to find out. The number 12065 is the zip code. Go to the post office and ask where zip code 12065 is, and the postal agent will tell you, "Oh, that's Clifton Park, New York." And of course, 0104 is my post office box number.

The sender of the envelope was named Rich, and he maintains an address of P.O. Box 104, Clifton Park, NY 12065.

If you decide to sue "Rich" for a deceptive act, which is discussed in the next chapters, you can even find the physical location of his business. When "Rich" applied for a P.O. Box, he had to complete an application with the postal authorities, and list his home and/or business address. The information on this application is sealed with the post office. The information used to be available under the Freedom of Information Act, but now restrictions apply, to prevent abusive husbands from hunting down wives who left them. However, a certified process server or lawyer can "break the box" and retrieve information from the application for the purpose of effectuating a lawsuit.

"Rich" may use this letter to set a caller ID trap. Debt collectors commonly use pen registers to trap phone numbers.

The letter inside the mysterious envelope may tell you to call a certain number. The number usually leads to a caller ID box. The purpose of the letter is to get you to call that number; and out of curiosity, you probably *will* call. After all, you don't know anyone by the name of Rich, and you want to know who sent you this letter.

Let's say the letter says to call 555-123-4567, and request extension 111. That's the number assigned to your account, although you don't know it. When you dial the number it connects you to a computer that asks you to enter the extension you want. The computer now has your phone number trapped, through caller ID. The debt collector will be calling within minutes, so be prepared.

Your number was trapped by deceptive means, and that is illegal. If you receive a mysterious letter requesting you to call a phone number, and the letter fails to provide the correct information, for example your account information, and the words, "This is an attempt to collect a debt and any information obtained will be used for that purpose," a violation of the FDCPA has occurred.

## BLOCKING CALLER ID

The Federal Trade Commission has ruled that if caller ID is legal, then consumers must at least be given an opportunity to have their number blocked from review.[2] Simply dialing *67 first, or 1167 for rotary phones, will block caller ID. However, this does not block ID on 800 or 888 numbers.

If you're afraid of your number being obtained, block the caller ID as outlined above. If the collection agency doesn't accept calls from "blocked" numbers, then communicate by writing; obviously they have a trap device waiting for your call.

Courts have routinely held that a consumer has no "right to privacy" in a phone number. Use of caller ID is legal. A debt collector may legally "trap" your phone number, and he does not even have to inform you that the number has been trapped. However, the communication the collector sends you requesting you to call a phone number must still comply with the FDCPA. These requirements are fully described in the next chapters.

## ADDITIONAL PLOYS

Skip-tracers sometimes set up a phantom corporation. This corporation will send the consumer a check, even for a small amount, under the guise that a prize had been won, or a refund issued. The consumer will deposit the check into their account. When the check is returned cashed to the phantom corporation, the name of the consumer's bank the check was deposited into is printed on the back—and the debt collector just found a bank account.

They also just violated the FDCPA, by using deceptive means to find you.

A phantom corporation can also pull your credit report. Debt collectors start a corporation, call it a "credit bureau," and do what they please with a consumer's credit report.

Another scam is for the debt collector to call your number and tell the person answering the phone that he is from a package carrier, and has to deliver a package to you. The unsuspecting person answering the phone blurts out your address, and suddenly the debt collector has your address.

And he violated the FDCPA, by being deceptive.

## SUMMARY

How a debt collector finds you is useful in combating him once the debt collection practice has begun.

It is permissible for the skip-tracer to:

1. call you, your neighbors, and your family;
2. identify himself;
3. state he is attempting to confirm your location;
4. identify his employer (if requested);
5. review your loan application and account documents for information;
6. call your other creditors;
7. review public record information, such as driving abstract and judgment information;
8. send you a letter with "Address Correction Requested," if the letter states the purpose of the communication, and identifies that it's from a debt collector; and
9. use caller ID.

It is *not* permissible for the skip-tracer to:

1. tell anyone you owe a debt;
2. call the same person more than once unless he believes the first response as to where you were was incomplete;
3. communicate by postcard;
4. use an envelope with a return address indicating the name of a collection agency;
5. talk to anyone after the debt collector knows you have an attorney;
6. use profane or misleading information in any conversations, with *anyone* they talk to; and
7. use any false or deceptive method to find you, including trapping you into calling a suspicious phone number, lying to get your address, causing you to deposit a check in an account, or using any other false and/or misleading method to locate you.

# CHAPTER 7

# REVIEWING THE FIRST LETTER

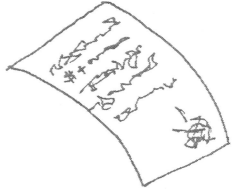

After the skip-tracer has found you, he will send your location information to the creditor or collection agency, and collection attempts will start. Remember, the law I am about to explain to you *only* applies to third-party collection agencies, pretend third-party collectors, skip-tracers, and law firms. If you are operating a business, the FDCPA does not apply; it only applies to consumer transactions. The FDCPA also does not apply to creditors acting in their own name.

## IMPERMISSIBLE FIRST LETTERS

Section 1692g of the FDCPA (Appendix I) tells you what language must be on the *first* letter the debt collector sends you.

The first letter must state:

"If you notify the debt collector in writing within the 30-day period that the debt, or any portion thereof, is disputed, or that the consumer requests the name and address of the original creditor, the debt collector shall cease collection of the debt, or any disputed portion thereof, until the debt collector obtains verification of the debt or a copy of the judgment, or the name and address of the original creditor, and a copy of such verification or judgment, or name and address of the original creditor, is mailed to the consumer by the debt collector."

This information *must* be contained in the first letter a debt collector sends to you. If this language is not in the letter, the debt collector has violated Section 1692g. Furthermore, if this language is not worded almost exactly as I have it here, an FDCPA violation has also occurred.

The wording of this notice requirement is a bit confusing. It simply means that if you notify the debt collector in writing, within 30 days of receipt of the letter, that you are disputing your debt or part of it, or that you want the name and address of the original creditor, the debt collector *must* stop collection until he mails you verification of the debt, or the name and address of the original creditor.

Remember, most collection agencies are not original creditors. They either bought the debt, or are collecting it for the original creditor for a fee.

If you do dispute the debt, make sure you do it in writing within 30 days of the first letter you receive. Send the letter certified, return receipt requested, so you can prove the date it was sent. If you *miss* the 30-day deadline, the debt is presumed to be valid.

You also must ask for identification of the original creditor within the same 30 days if the account was sold. If you receive a collection letter from a company you never had a loan or credit card with, your creditor probably sold the account.

If you send that letter out within 30 days from the date of the collection letter, the collection agency must cease collection until it provides you with the information requested. If they continue to attempt to collect the debt before validating the debt or informing you of the identity of the original creditor, they violated the FDCPA and you can sue the agency.

When debt collectors first learned of this requirement, they started all types of little tricks. They put the notice on the back of their letters where no one would see it. They printed it in really small letters so no one could read it. They printed it in very faint type, so that the demand section of the letter, printed in bolder type, "overshadowed" the mandatory language. The consumer's attention is thus drawn to the bold demand for payment, possibly causing them to miss the words telling them they have an inherent right to dispute any debt.

All of these tricks have been held by the courts to be illegal. The language of this notice must be *clearly legible and visible.* It cannot be faintly printed, with the language demanding payment overshadowing it with bolder print. Overshadowing can be an FDCPA violation.

Also, if this notice is on the back of the letter, the front of the letter must tell you, "See Reverse for Important Information." This note to see the warning on the other side of the letter also cannot be in faint or tiny print or overshadowed by the rest of the letter.

There is additional wording that is required to be on *all* collection letters (including the first one). *Every* collection letter must state this sentence: "This is an attempt to collect a debt and any information obtained will be used for that purpose." If a collection letter doesn't state that information, a violation of the FDCPA has occurred, and you can sue the agency.

## THE ENVELOPE

It is illegal to send a collection letter in an envelope that indicates it was sent by a debt collector. Even though the substance of the letter indicates your right to dispute the debt, the envelope cannot have the name of a debt collector in the return address box. The envelope also cannot be transparent. You have a right to privacy, and the world should not know that a debt collector is trying to contact you.

A debt collector's name can be on the return address, but only if is not obviously the name of a collection agency.

Following are some examples of correct and incorrect collection letters. Letters 1) and 2) are correct. They both indicate the account balance and amount due, and contain all the language that Section 1692g tells us should be in a first letter.

## LETTER 1)

*CORRECT (PROPER INFORMATION AND WORDING)*

Bilgewater Collections
POB 999
Sharksville, NY 98765

J. Smith
Main Street
Anytown, USA

Re: credit card acct. number: 12345
Balance due: $171.25

Dear J. Smith:

Your account was referred to me for collection. I would like to resolve this dispute to everyone's satisfaction.

Please forward payment within thirty (30) days.

In the event of questions, please do not hesitate to contact me.

Very truly yours,

*C. Bass.*

If you notify the debt collector in writing within the 30 day period that the debt, or any portion thereof, is disputed, or that the consumer requests the name and address of the original creditor, the debt collector shall cease collection of the debt, or any disputed portion thereof, until the debt collector obtains verification of the debt or a copy of the judgment, or the name and address of the original creditor, and a copy of such veri-fication or judgment, or name and address of the original creditor, is mailed to the consumer by the debt collector.

This is an attempt to collect a debt, and any information obtained will be used for that purpose.

## CORRECT (PROPER INFORMATION AND WORDING)

Bilgewater Collections
POB 999
Sharksville, NY 98765

J. Smith
Main Street
Anytown, USA

Re: credit card acct. number: 12345
Balance due: $171.25

Dear J. Smith:

Your account was referred to me for collection. I would like to resolve this dispute to everyone's satisfaction.

Please forward payment within thirty (30) days.

In the event of questions, please do not hesitate to contact me.

Very truly yours,

*C. Bass.*

### See Reverse Side for Important Consumer Information!

(REVERSE SIDE)

If you notify the debt collector in writing within the 30 day period . . . (etc.)

This is an attempt to collect a debt . . . (etc.)

*INCORRECT (OVERSHADOWING)*

Bilgewater Collections
POB 999
Sharksville, NY 98765

J. Smith
Main Street
Anytown, USA

Re: credit card acct. number: 12345
Balance due: $171.25

Dear J. Smith:

**Your account was referred to me for collection. I would like to resolve this dispute to everyone's satisfaction.**

**Please forward payment within thirty (30) days.**

Very truly yours,

*C. Bass.*

See reverse side for important information.

**(REVERSE SIDE)**

If you notify the debt collector in writing within the 30 day period . . . (etc.)

This is an attempt to collect a debt . . . (etc.)

### INCORRECT (LANGUAGE MISSING)

Bilgewater Collections
POB 999
Sharkville, NY 98765

J. Smith
Main Street
Anytown, USA

Re: credit card acct. number: 12345
Balance due: $171.25

Dear J. Smith:

Your account was referred to me for collection. I would like to resolve this dispute to everyone's satisfaction.

Please forward payment within seven (7) days.

Very truly yours,

*C. Bass.*

## DISPUTED DEBTS

Section 1692g also tells you how to dispute the debt. If you believe you do not owe a debt, you must tell the collection agency that you dispute it. You can certainly tell them over the phone, but we all know phone records mysteriously disappear. Write a letter to the collection agency, explain why you do not think you owe the money, and send supporting documentation. Do not send original paperwork; it may disappear. Make photocopies of everything.

Be sure to send the letter to the agency by certified mail, return receipt requested. The certified receipt, and especially the signed confirmation that the post office sends back to you with the signature that the letter was received, all become part of the log you will keep.

The collection agency must "verify" your debt before it commences additional collection efforts. If the slip you receive back from the post office indicates that your letter was received, for example, on August 5, and on August 14th you receive a debt collection letter or call, the collection agency has violated the FDCPA and you may sue them.

On the dispute letter clearly state your name, address, and the date of the letter. Be sure to include the address of the collection agency and your account number, or the collection agency reference number. You do not have to provide a phone number. If you omit the phone number, then you are forcing the collection agency to respond to your dispute in writing. You would rather receive verification of your debt by the collection agency in writing than over the phone; remember, in a phone conversation, it's your word against the collection agency's word. In writing, you have solid evidence of the dispute.

*SAMPLE DISPUTE LETTER*

J. Smith
Main Street,
Anytown, USA

August 1, 2001

C. Bass
Bilgewater Collections
POB 999
Sharkville, NY 98765

Re: credit card acct. number: 12345
Balance: $171.25

Dear Mr. Bass:

I am in receipt of your collection letter dated July 1, 2001. At this time I am disputing the debt. I do not recall ever having a debt with the Scrooge National Bank, and believe you have me confused with my ex-wife. PLEASE VERIFY THIS DEBT IMMEDIATELY.

Sincerely,

*Joe Smith*

The requirement of Section 1692g, the debt verification notice, " . . . is designed to fulfill congressional intent to 'eliminate the recurring problem of debt collectors dunning the wrong person or attempting to collect debts which the consumer has already paid.'"[3]

If the consumer disputes the debt in writing, " . . . the debt collector shall cease collection of the debt, or any disputed portion thereof, until the debt collector obtains verification of the debt or a copy of the judgment, and a copy of such verification is mailed to the consumer."[4] Section 1692g(b) thus gives debt collectors two options when they receive requests for validation; they may provide the requested validation and continue their debt collection activities or they may cease all collection activities.[5]

When a debt collector cannot verify a debt, the statute allows the debt collector to cease all collection activities without incurring any liability for the mistake. However, the court case *Rabideau v. Management Adjustment Bureau*[6] decided, "If the consumer disputes the debt or requests, in writing, the name of the original creditor, then the creditor must halt all collection efforts until it mails verification of the debt."

Make a little note in your collection journal. Although the language states that you have 30 days to dispute the debt, the language does not say the collection agency must send you the information requested *within* 30 days. Courts are split on what the collection agency must do, but the majority opinion states that the collection agency must cease all collection activity until the requested verification information is sent to you.

When the collection agency receives your request for verification, it sends the request to its client. That client may be the original creditor, who then must hunt down all your original documents, and supply copies to you.

However, the collection agency's client may be a purchaser that purchased your debt from the original creditor. The purchaser is also a debt collector, and must comply with the same request for verification.

The more verification requests you send certified, the more support you have for your case when the collection agency fails to verify your debt.

## PROPER VERIFICATION

Make sure the collection agency sends you the correct verification. A classic example of a disputed debt is "stolen identity." Stolen-identity cases arise often in divorce cases, when one spouse opens charge accounts in the other spouse's name, and runs up bills. Unfortunately, if you're living apart from each other, your spouse may have the bills going to another address altogether. In short, you may not know that your ex-spouse opened an account in your name until the bill has not been paid for months, and the damage to your credit report is already done.

When you dispute your debt in a theft-of-identity case, the collection agency usually sends you nothing more than an accounting of the transactions. *This is insufficient.* You want to see if the signature on the charges and the account application match *your* signature. Write the collection agency until it provides this information. A charge history with no proof of signature is of little value to you.

## HOW MUCH DO YOU OWE?

Section 1692g also describes the collection agency's responsibility to inform you how *much* you owe. In the initial collection letter, or within five (5) days thereafter, the collection agency must tell you both the amount of the debt, and who you owe the money to.

## OWING MORE THAN ONE DEBT

If you owe more than one debt, and you make a payment, the debt collector cannot apply the payment to a disputed debt. He must apply the payment to whatever debt you desire.

## THE DISPUTED DEBT AND YOUR CREDIT REPORT

I discuss this in length later in the book. However, if you disputed your debt, the debt collector must list the debt as disputed on your credit report. This requirement is for your protection. Debt collectors love to stick derogatory information about consumers on credit reports. If derogatory information from a collection agency is on your credit report, the fact that you disputed the debt must also be listed. [Appendix I, Section 1692e(8)] If your dispute is not on the credit report, you can sue the collection agency.

## CONFLICTING PAYMENT DEMANDS

As you know, a consumer has 30 days to dispute a debt. Many collection agencies will demand payment in fewer than 30 days. A demand for payment in less than 30 days violates section 1692g of the FDCPA. For example, if the letter states, "You must pay in five (5) days," and then proceeds with the language of section 1692g, which states that the consumer has 30 days to dispute the debt, a violation of the FDCPA has occurred. This was decided in the court case of *Russell v. Equifax.*[7]

The reason is that consumers will be confused by the letter's wording; they're told they have 30 days to dispute the debt, but must pay it within five days.

## MORE THAN ONE LETTER IN 30 DAYS

The facts of *Russell* are even more interesting, as it examines the situation where multiple letters were sent. The first letter was adequate and complied with Section 1692g, giving the consumer 30 days to dispute the debt. A second letter was sent 10 days later, demanding payment in five days. The court held the *combination* of letters to be illegal, because they will confuse a consumer. The first letter provided the consumer with the proper 30-day period to dispute the debt; the second letter, sent shortly after the first, demanded payment *within* the 30-day dispute period.

A critical point to be aware of in the application of the *Russell* decision: Be sure to examine not just the first letter, but *all* letters sent after the first one as well, which demand payment within the 30-day time frame. (In the *Russell* case, the collector violated both Section 1692g and Section 1692e(10).)

Letter 6) is a classic example of a *Russell* violation. It violates the law for several reasons, some of which will be discussed later. (See *Threat of Unintended Action* in Chapter 5.)

You have 30 days to dispute a debt. If the collection agency demands payment within that 30 days, the FDCPA is violated. In example 6), payment is demanded in seven days. The letter *cannot* demand payment in less than 30 days. If it demands payment in *any* number of days less than the 30-day dispute period, you can sue the collection agency based on that demand.

Courts have *repeatedly held for the consumer* in this situation.

*INCORRECT (DEMANDS PAYMENT IN LESS THAN 30 DAYS)*

Bilgewater Collections
POB 999
Sharksville, NY 98765

August 1, 2001

J. Smith
Main Street
Anytown, USA

Re: credit card acct. number: 12345
Balance due: $171.25

Dear J. Smith:

Your account was referred to me for collection. We are demanding payment within seven (7) days. Please remit payment for $171.25 within seven (7) days to avoid further action.

Please forward payment within seven days.

Very truly yours,

*C. Bass.*

If you notify the debt collector in writing within the 30 day period . . . (etc.)

This is an attempt to collect a debt . . . (etc.)

This rule also applies to multiple letters sent within the first 30-day time period.

For example, see letters 7) and 8). Letter 7), sent August 1, 2001, demands payment in 30 days. Letter 8), dated August 14, 2001, demands payment in seven days. Letter 7) is legal (except for the threat of "further action," which will be discussed later). However, it is superseded by the second letter, which demands payment in less than 30 days, and that demand overrides the first letter.

## THE LETTER/PHONE CALL COMBINATION

The debt collector will usually send you the first demand letter, and then follow up with a phone call.

Fortunately, the 30-day rule also applies to combinations of letter/telephone contacts. If you receive a letter properly providing you with 30 days to dispute the debt, the debt collector *cannot* call you and demand, over the phone, payment before the 30 days has lapsed.

Let's say the debt collector sent you a demand letter on August 1, 2001, introducing himself and providing you with the requisite 30 days to dispute the debt. On August 7th, the debt collector calls you and inquires as to when they may receive payment. You respond that you do not get paid again until Friday, August 14th. The debt collector then *demands* payment at that time. A violation of the FDCPA has occurred.

Notice that I used the word "demand." An FDCPA violation does not necessarily occur if the debt collector *requests* payment within the 30 days.

Any demand for payment, or combination of demands for payment, in less than the initial 30-day right-to-dispute period, is a violation of the FDCPA, as seen in letter 6) and 7).

### INCORRECT (DEMANDS PAYMENT WITHIN 30 DAYS)

Bilgewater Collections
POB 999
Sharksville, NY 98765

August 1, 2001

J. Smith
Main Street
Anytown, USA

Re: credit card acct. number: 12345
Balance due: $171.25

Dear J. Smith:

Your account was referred to me for collection. We are demanding payment within thirty (30) days. Please remit payment for $171.25 within thirty (30) days to avoid further action.

Very truly yours,

*C. Bass.*

If you notify the debt collector in writing within the 30-day period . . . (etc.)

This is an attempt to collect a debt . . . (etc.)

*INCORRECT (WHEN FOLLOWING LETTER 7)*

Bilgewater Collections
POB 999
Sharksville, NY 98765

August 14, 2001

J. Smith
Main Street
Anytown, USA

Re: credit card acct. number: 12345
Balance due: $171.25

Dear J. Smith:

I wrote you two weeks ago, and still I have not received payment. Your creditor is extremely upset over your inaction. I have been authorized to give you seven (7) more days to voluntarily pay, before I take further action to collect on this debt.

Please forward payment within seven (7) days.

Very truly yours,

*C. Bass.*

If you notify the debt collector in writing within the 30 day period . . . (etc.)

This is an attempt to collect a debt . . . (etc.)

# ✔ CHECKLIST

☐ Does your first letter state almost verbatim the following? "If you notify the debt collector in writing within the 30 day period that the debt, or any portion thereof, is disputed, or that the consumer requests the name and address of the original creditor, the debt collector shall cease collection of the debt, or any disputed portion thereof, until the debt collector obtains verification of the debt or a copy of the judgment, or the name and address of the original creditor, and a copy of such verification or judgment, or name and address of the original creditor, is mailed to the consumer by the debt collector. This is an attempt to collect a debt and any information obtained will be used for that purpose."

☐ Is the language above "overshadowed" by other language in the letter? That is, is the demand part of your letter in bold print, while the mandatory disclosure is faint or illegible

☐ If the mandatory language is on the back of the letter, does the letter tell you to "See Reverse for Important Information"?

☐ Did the letter arrive in an envelope that was clearly from a collection agency?

☐ Did you dispute the letter, in writing, within 30 days?

☐ Did the collection agency note your dispute on your credit report?

☐ Did the collection agency "verify" your debt—that is, send you the information you disputed—*before* sending additional collection letters, or placing collection calls?

❑ Does the letter demand payment *within* 30 days, even though providing you with a full 30 days to dispute the debt?

❑ Did the debt collector send you more than one letter in the first 30 days, demanding payment before the 30 day right-to-dispute period has expired?

❑ Did the debt collector provide you with the proper 30 days to dispute the debt, and then demand payment before the 30 days was up, by a phone call/letter combination?

# GENERAL PROHIBITIONS ON CONTACT

## *COLLECTION COMMUNICATION*

In Chapter 4 we examined mandatory language requirements for the first letter sent to you. This chapter examines language in phone calls and letters —including the first letter—which is unlawful. While Chapter 4 tells us what language the FDCPA says *must* be present, this chapter helps us examine the other language in the body of the letters. In short, this chapter helps us find out what should not be in letters, or any other communications with you.

Section 1692c of the FDCPA (Appendix I) is entitled "Communication in connection with debt collection." This section covers both written and oral communications with the consumer.

The debt collector will most likely have sent you a first demand letter before calling you. The language in the first demand letter, and, of course, your right to dispute the debt and demand verification, is governed by the 30-day rule. Once the 30 days is past, we will assume the phone calls, and more demand letters, will start.

The blanket prohibitions in Section 1692c are straightforward, but certainly demand review nonetheless. The law addresses the agency's "contact" with you. This means mainly writings and phone calls. However, Section 1692c refers to *any* contact, and with modern technology it could arguably include e-mail.

## PERMISSIBLE PHONE CONTACT

Section 1692a(1) states that the debt collector may not call you at any unusual place or time that he knows is inconvenient to you.

If the debt collector does not know whether the time or place is inconvenient, he should not call you between 8 a.m. and 9 p.m.

If you work the graveyard shift, from midnight to 8 in the morning, you have every right to tell the debt collector not to call you during the day. When you communicate that to the debt collector, he must enter that information in your account information, and *not* contact you at the time specified. The caveat for triggering a violation under this section is that the debt collector must *know* he cannot call you at a certain time or place.

The debt collector is faced with a dilemma when he receives your request. The typical collection agency handles so many accounts that it uses an automated computerized dialing system. The account information of thousands of consumers is downloaded into a computer, and the computer automatically dials telephone numbers. When a number is dialed, the debt collector's computer screen lights up with the account information.

When you send a particular request, for example to not call during the day, to the debt collector, your account information must be retrieved from the computer banks. The debt collector thereafter must manually pull your file, and manually dial your number at an appropriate time.

All communications you have with the debt collector addressing limitations on contact with you should be placed in the journal you are by now keeping. Also, send the request in writing, certified, return receipt requested. Always keep a copy of the letter. You can easily determine a breach in this request by reviewing the debt collector's phone records. If you receive a call at an inopportune time or place, a violation of the FDCPA has occurred. (Letter 9.)

## CALLING AT INAPPROPRIATE PLACES

The debt collector also cannot call you at an inconvenient place. If you do not want to be called at work, tell the debt collector that. A debt collector may contact you at work. However, the debt collector may not contact you at work if he knows your employer does not allow such calls. [Appendix I, Section 1692c(a)(3)]

The concept of receiving calls at an "inconvenient place" can arise under many circumstances. For example, if you work on an assembly line and receive a call, you can't easily leave the assembly line to answer the phone. If you're a doctor in an emergency room, you can't easily leave the emergency room to answer a phone.

If you're visiting your mother in another city and tell the debt collector where you are during the "friendly" conversation I warned you about earlier, the debt collector may locate your mother and call you there on Saturday morning. Her number is easy to locate; the collector has her maiden name and can trace virtually all of your relatives. Letter 9) is a typical "no contact" letter. Do *not* tell the debt collector where you work! If debt collection activity rises to the level of you being sued, the debt collector now knows where to garnish your wages.

## CALLING WHEN YOU HAVE AN ATTORNEY

If you retain the services of an attorney to handle your debt, let the debt collector know immediately. Section 1692c(a)(2), makes it unlawful for the debt collector to contact you—whether by writing or phone—if they know you have an attorney. The debt collector must know the attorney's name, address, and phone number, or must be able to readily ascertain that information.

Inform your attorney to immediately send a letter of representation to the debt collector.

If your attorney later fails to return the debt collector's calls, then the debt collector may start contacting you again.

J. Smith
Main Street
Anytown, USA

September 5, 2001
CERTIFIED – RETURN RECEIPT REQUESTED

C. Bass
Bilgewater Collections
POB 999
Sharksville, NY 98765

Re: credit card acct. number: 12345
Balance due: $171.25

Dear Mr. Bass:

Yesterday you called me at 9 a.m. in the morning. I work the midnight to 8 a.m. shift; therefore, please do not call me days. A daytime phone call is very inconvenient for me, because that is when I am sleeping. You also have my work number. Kindly do not contact me at work.

Thank you in advance for your courtesy.

Sincerely,

*J. Smith*

A consumer will typically inform the debt collector he or she is filing bankruptcy, and provide the debt collector with the name and address of the attorney representing them. The debt collector should thereafter cease communication with you. Situations have arisen where the debt collector tells the consumer, "I don't care if you have an attorney," or, "I don't care if you're filing bankruptcy." This language violates the FDCPA. One of these statements spoken just one time is sufficient to trigger a violation. Tell your attorney. If you already did file for bankruptcy protection, the bankruptcy laws provide additional avenues of relief.

## COMMUNICATION WITH THIRD PARTIES

The debt collector (or skip-tracer) can legally call third parties—your friends, neighbors, or relatives—if he's trying to *locate* you. If the call is to find you for the first time, he must:

1. identify himself;
2. state he is confirming your location; and
3. identify his employer (if requested).

The debt collector cannot:

1. tell anyone you owe a debt;
2. call the same person more than once, unless he believes the first response as to where you were was incomplete;
3. communicate by postcard;
4. Use an envelope with a return address indicating the name of a collection agency; and
5. talk to *anyone* after he knows you have an attorney.

Debt collectors love to call parents and inform them their son or daughter is a deadbeat and not paying their bills. *This is unlawful.*

Except to find you, the debt collector cannot discuss your debt with anyone except you, your attorney, his attorney, a credit reporting agency, or his client, the creditor. The only exception to this is if you are a minor; then the collector may talk to your parents.

If the debt collector is communicating with a third party with whom they *can* legally discuss the claim (i.e., a spouse or parent of a minor, or a permitted third party), whether by writing or verbally, they must *still* make the disclosures in Section 1692g, that they are attempting to collect a debt, and any information obtained will be used for that purpose. In addition, they cannot lawfully harass the person they're communicating with. In other words, the same FDCPA protections that apply to you *also* apply to the other folks the collector is calling. These third parties have the same protections you have against abuse, harassment, and deceptive acts and practices.

## STOPPING COMMUNICATION FROM THE COLLECTOR

Section 1692c(c) is extremely important if you don't want *any* communication with the debt collector. Section 1692c(c) specifically states that if you advise the debt collector, in writing, that you refuse to pay a debt, or do not want further communication with him, he must cease *all* communications with you, both written and verbal.

The debt collector can only communicate with you thereafter to acknowledge your request, to inform you further communication will not be made, and to notify you that his agency may be invoking "particular remedies." In short, that they will sue you.

## *YOU MAY NOT WANT COMMUNICATION TO CEASE*

If you *do* notify the collector, by letter or phone, to stop sending you mail and calling you, by law they must stop. This sounds like an incredibly easy way to resolve your collection issue. But the problem lies in what the debt collector's *next* step is. If the account is worth pursuing—and there's no way to determine that—the debt collector may see your avoidance as a sign to "ripen" the collection to the next level. That level is a lawsuit. Since you are refusing to negotiate with the collector, he may turn the account over to a law firm. The firm will then sue you, and attempt to use state collection remedies to collect on the debt.

# HARASSMENT
# AND ABUSE

**S**ection 1692d of the FDCPA says that a debt collector may not harass or abuse you.

I have stated repeatedly that collection agencies thrive on the concept I call "power over." Because you owe them money, they supposedly have power over you. If you are having financial difficulties, chances are something bad happened in your life, such as loss of a job, a relationship, or your health, and your feelings of self worth may be low. The collector will often try to make you feel even worse about yourself, which gives him more "power over" you. One way to do this is by harassing and abusing you.

I have also stated that the collection industry usually works on a contingency fee arrangement with the creditor. This fee varies. Twenty years ago the collector could keep perhaps as much as half of what he collected. Today the fees have been drastically reduced, due to increased competition. On some large accounts, the lowest bidder receives the collection assignment. Some fees may be as low as 5%. At this rate, the collection agency only makes $50 for every $1,000 they collect. While this seems incredibly low, the agency hopes to offset it by the high volume of business from large accounts like hospitals.

When a collector joins such an agency, he's usually provided with a copy of a collection manual. This manual instructs him on the FDCPA, and defines what constitutes unlawful conduct. However, because the agency depends on a high volume of collections, it often gives the collector free reign to collect as much money as possible, in any way he sees fit. The consumers' FDCPA rights are often tossed aside.

Although Section 1692d of the FDCPA protects consumers from harassment or abuse, certainly a lot of consumers continue to get harassed or abused. Most collectors believe they *do* have power over the consumer, and this leads many collectors to believe they can say and do whatever they want. The mean and oppressive comments that collectors say to people are rarely found in a training manual; sadly, they come from the collector's heart. We are left to wonder what type of person is mean to someone who may be on the brink of losing their home because of an uninsured medical situation or job layoff.

Section 1692d lists six items that constitute "harassment." The items listed are only examples. The list of violations is not exhaustive. *Any* harassment or abuse is unlawful. If you feel a debt collector has harassed you, the law may have been broken regardless of whether the offense is listed or not.

The listed offenses are as follows.

The debt collector may not:

1. use violence or the threat of violence to harm you, your property, or your reputation [Section 1692d(1)];
2. use obscene or profane language to you [Section 1692d(2)];

3. "publish" your name as someone who does not pay their bills;
4. advertise the sale of your debt;
5. call you so many times you're ready to pull your hair out;
6. call you and not tell you who they are.

The statute does not specifically define what behavior constitutes "harassment" or "abuse." Each case must be evaluated separately. If you feel you have been harassed by a collector, call an attorney, and report it to the Attorney General of your state.

Here are some examples that the courts have held constituted harassment. A collector called a consumer a "deadbeat," a "crook," and a "liar."[8]

A collector told a woman she shouldn't have children if she couldn't afford to pay the hospital bill for them.[9]

One collector told a consumer, "No more false promises." This too was declared harassment.[10]

My personal favorite example of outrageous abuse came from a 39-year-old woman who had been diagnosed with brain cancer. The collector worked for the actual creditor, not a collection agency. Therefore the FDCPA did not apply, but the woman sued under the tort of Intentional Infliction of Emotional Distress.

The client had had surgery to remove the tumor. After the surgery she was wheelchair-bound, and suffered from temporary blindness. She forgot to make her car payment.

When the collector called, the woman explained her situation and promised to eventually make good on her car payment. She just needed time to recover. But the collector would not take "No" for an answer. He told her he would just, quote, " . . . put a lien against your house, and get my money when you're dead." This happened in the 1990s, so don't think such behavior is outdated.

Some collectors actually threaten consumers with physical harm. Believe it or not, some collectors have made bomb threats against consumers. One collector sent a letter with a depiction of a decapitated man on it. The letter read, in part, "If you think what we have been writing is unpleasant, don't challenge us to see what happens if you keep avoiding us." This was a clear violation of the FDCPA.

The harassment and abuse does not have to be just verbal. The debt collector cannot repeatedly phone you, time and time again. The number of calls that constitute harassment varies depending on circumstances, but as a general rule, multiple calls within a single day can be considered harassment. Cases exist where the debt collector called the consumer 10 times in 30 minutes! This legally constituted harassment and abuse. In some cases even two calls are enough, if the second one comes after you've asked the collector not to call again.

Repeated mailings may also constitute harassment and abuse. If you receive many debt collection letters, or get bombarded with summonses in the mail, call an attorney immediately.

Computerized, automated systems can cause legal troubles for collectors because they sometimes generate call after call, or letter after letter, in a short period of time.

Collectors also may not publish the fact that you did not pay a bill. There are exceptions to this. Non-payment may be reported to a credit reporting agency. Also, if you get sued and have a judgment against you, or if you have filed bankruptcy, these items are public record. Newspapers routinely publish lists of people who filed bankruptcy. Usually, however, the papers publish only the names of businesses that filed.

Again, the FDCPA does not define harassment. For guidance, we have to look at what behavior the courts have held to be harassment. However, your feelings can usually be trusted. If you *feel* that you have been harassed or abused, you probably have been. Call your lawyer.

Your parents and spouses and significant others are also protected from this prohibition against harassment.

# CHAPTER 10

# FALSE AND MISLEADING REPRESENTATIONS

A debt collector may not make false and misleading representations. Section 1692e of the FDCPA lists 12 factors that are illegal because they are "false or misleading." However, this list is not exhaustive. If a collection agency did something to you that you think is false or misleading, consult with a consumer protection lawyer to determine whether your rights have been violated. The law is intentionally broad, to accommodate any number of schemes a collector may try to trick you with. Just because a trick a collector pulled on you is not on the list, does not mean the conduct was legal.

Determining whether something in a collector's conduct, or his language in a letter or phone call, is "false and misleading," is not as obvious as it seems.

To begin with, a debt collector cannot:

1. imply he is from, or supported by, the Federal Government; or
2. misrepresent the character, amount, or status of the debt.

This language needs clarification.

## MISREPRESENTATION OF STATUS

The debt collector may not misrepresent the status of the debt. For example, if you have not been sued, a debt collector cannot tell you he has a *judgment* against you. As I told you before, a debt collector is limited to calling you and sending you letters requesting payment. If calls and letters don't work, the collector can refer your account to an attorney, and *they* can sue you. Once an attorney sues you and wins (obtains a judgment), the law allows for other methods of debt collection. These extra judicial remedies vary broadly from state to state, but they may include garnishing your wages, freezing your bank account, and attaching a lien to your home.

If a collector tells you he will garnish your wages, freeze your bank account, or attach a lien on your house—and you have *not* been sued—then the collector has violated the FDCPA by misrepresenting the status of your debt. He implied a post-judgment remedy, when, in fact, he has not even determined whether to sue you or not.

## MISREPRESENTATION OF AMOUNT DUE

A debt collector is not allowed to misrepresent the "amount due." This misrepresentation can arise in a number of situations, but it often occurs in the balance of your account, and if you filed bankruptcy. The bankruptcy factor arises because after bankruptcy, the balance of your account is zero.

This factor may arise in the context of a *lien*. A typical scenario is what happens with "after acquired property."

For example, let's say you get sued in 1995, and the court finds in favor of the creditor. You own no real property (no home). That's good, because a judgment—at least in New York State—operates as a lien against your home. A judgment *automatically* attaches to your home, just like a second mortgage.

One important caveat exists: Your home must have enough equity in it to allow the lien in. If your home is worth $100,000, and you have a first mortgage of $80,000 and a second mortgage for $20,000, there is no equity left. If a hospital sues you for an unpaid $20,000 bill, that judgment does not "attach" itself to your home because there isn't any equity to accommodate it. (In this case, if you were to file bankruptcy, the judgment is *discharged*.)

If you did not have that second mortgage, however, and had only the $80,000 mortgage on your $100,000 home, that $20,000 hospital judgment attaches itself to your home as a lien. You cannot sell your house until the lien is paid off. It sits there forever.

But let's say you *did* have that second mortgage of $20,000, and the lien cannot attach to the house because there's no equity. As you gradually pay on both mortgages, and develop equity in the house, the lien *does* begin to attach. For every dollar of equity you earn, the lien is attached for that amount, until the entire $20,000 judgment exists as a lien.

Some states have a statute of limitation on judgments, and it varies from state to state. In New York it's 20 years.

An interesting situation arises in the context of "after acquired property."

If you were sued, and judgment entered, and you do not own a home, you obviously do not have to worry about a lien against a home. (Although you do have to worry about other methods of collection.) But if you buy a home five years later, the lien automatically attaches.

What happens, however, if you filed bankruptcy *after* the judgment was entered, but *before* you bought a home?

The judgment, sitting dormant in the county, city, or town clerk's office, changed into a lien when you purchased your home. Perhaps you discovered the lien when you went to refinance the home. You called the debt collector who obtained the judgment, and explained to him that the underlying debt was discharged in bankruptcy. The collector shrugs his shoulders and says he can't help you.

This is arguably an FDCPA violation on the part of the law firm that got the judgment against you. By keeping a lien against your house, the lien is misrepresenting the amount of the debt. The debt is zero because it was discharged, whereas the lien is for a "sum certain" (a specific amount). This may also be a violation of various bankruptcy laws; however, make sure bankruptcy laws do not preempt the FDPCA in your jurisdiction.

## CREDIT REPORT MISREPRESENTATION

Debt collectors love to place information regarding your delinquent account on your credit report. This collection method is particularly useful when the debt is too small to sue you for. The credit report will reflect the account as unpaid, and you will not be able to obtain new credit until the delinquent account is paid in full.

After you file bankruptcy, the amount of the debt is "zero." A collector must reflect this zero balance on your credit report. Will the debt collector make the required changes to your credit report? Of course not! A computer is doing all the work, while the collector is playing golf, and he is more interested in suing on new accounts than correcting errors on old ones anyway.

If you want to correct this error, you'll have to dispute it yourself. Write to the credit reporting agency, telling them the correct amount (zero), and send a carbon copy to the original creditor. If the issue isn't resolved in 30 days, you can sue the creditor and the credit reporting agency, under federal and state credit reporting law.

There are other illegal misrepresentations. The debt collector may not:

1. say he's an attorney, or from a law office, unless he really is;

2. say that if you don't pay the debt you'll go to prison; or
3. threaten an action he has no intention of taking.

## MISREPRESENTATION OF LEGAL STATUS

If a collector says he's an attorney, or from a law office, ask him what law firm he's from. If you don't believe him, contact the Court Administration Office in your state to prove he's an attorney. If he isn't, a violation of the FDCPA has occurred.

## THREAT OF PRISON

This absurd and mean practice has been outlawed in all 50 states for many years. If a debt collector threatens you with jail time, an outrageous violation of the FDCPA has occurred.

## THREAT OF UNINTENDED ACTION

A *lot* of litigation has occurred under Section 1692e(5 and 10), and most of the results have been entirely pro-consumer.

A Section 1692e(5 and 10) violation is very difficult to uncover. When you, the consumer, are reading your debt collection letters, you probably never thought some of the language in that letter rose to the level of a lawsuit. All the litigation centers around what it means to "threaten an action the collector has no intention of taking."

The real interesting litigation is in the words that have been *interpreted* to mean a lawsuit is going to be brought against you. If a collector makes a threat to "take an action against you," the courts have interpreted this to mean he is threatening to sue you. And if you are threatened with a lawsuit, and the collector has no *intention* of suing you, a violation has occurred.

You must first understand how a collector goes about deciding whether to sue you.

Only the creditor or owner of the debt can actually decide to sue; after all, it's their debt. The collector must first obtain *permission* to sue from the creditor. If the collector has sent you a few letters, and you never responded, the collector must contact the creditor and recommend suing you. The creditor must agree to a suit, and then a law firm that specializes in "creditor's rights" is contacted. A fee is agreed upon, and the original creditor forwards the law firm the expenses of the lawsuit.

The important thing to understand is this: The collector cannot, *on his own, without prior authority,* decide to sue you.

Therefore, before permission to sue you is obtained from the creditor, a collector cannot, either orally or in writing, threaten to sue you.

When I use the words, "threaten to sue you," I do not mean just the obvious language of, "I am going to sue you." The analysis is not so simple.

We must look at four separate factors:

1. the language of the letter;
2. the balance due;
3. whether the letter is computer-generated; and
4. whether you were actually sued within a "reasonable" period of time after the threat was made.

## LANGUAGE OF THE LETTER

If the letter states non-payment will result in "further action," and no further action, like a lawsuit, occurs, you can sue the debt collector. The words "further action" or "immediate action" or "legal action" have *all* been legally interpreted to mean an impending lawsuit. If no lawsuit is filed, this threat is a "threat of action not intended to be taken," and is therefore an FDCPA violation. This has been tested many times in the courts. To quote the court in one of these cases, "Language in collection letter which could be interpreted as requiring that debt be paid within five (5) days to avoid 'further action' could be interpreted by the least sophisticated consumer as a threat to commence legal action, of kind which the debt collector did not have authority to take."[11]

The courts in these cases have held that the least sophisticated consumer will interpret "further action" or "immediate action" to mean lawsuit. These phrases *imply* the imminence of a lawsuit.

If no lawsuit is contemplated when the letter is sent, a violation has occurred, because the collector has threatened an action (a lawsuit) which he did not have the authority to take.

Obviously, if the consumer is actually sued, the threat is not an empty one.

What is a "reasonable" amount of time to sue after the threat to sue? You should hear from a lawyer within a month. As a legal practitioner, I generally draw a line in the sand if no notification of a lawsuit is received after 30 days has passed since the threat to take action.

## COMPUTER-GENERATED LETTERS

Courts have repeatedly held that a lawyer who is threatening to sue must review and analyze each *separate* account involved, and then make a qualified decision whether to recommend suit. Unfortunately for the debt collector, such individualized review is rarely possible when maintaining a volume business. A lawyer cannot review thousands of files a day. As I told you, account information is downloaded into a computer. The computer also sends letters! The program is set up to send a letter to you every specific number of days, for example, every 30 days. Every time a 30-day period expires, the computer automatically churns out a newer, harsher letter. The collector's signature is stamped on the bottom.

If the letter threatens "further action," or "immediate action," the courts have interpreted that to mean the attorney has made an *individualized decision* to sue you. If no such decision has been made, the threat is a false threat, and is a violation of the FDCPA. Without an individual review, it is impossible to determine whether an honest, objective conclusion had been reached to file suit.

In the lawsuit *Clomon v. Jackson*,[12] the court stated, "No mass mailing technique with respect to debt collection letters is permissible, regardless of how effective it might be, if the technique constitutes false, deceptive, or misleading communication." Computers churn out one letter after the next. Is it possible for the attorney who owns the system to review thousands, perhaps millions, of accounts?

If you receive a letter or phone call, threatening a lawsuit, or threatening "further action," you may have a lawsuit against the collection agency if you are not sued within a "reasonable period of time." As I said above, that's normally within 30 days, and 60 days for sure.

## SMALL BALANCES

Collectors also rarely sue on balances less than $500. I won't say as a blanket rule that if the balance is less than $500 you won't get sued, but it's rare. Rarer yet is getting sued on an account of, say, $8. I have seen collectors threaten "further action" on an $8 bill! Obviously, a creditor will think twice before expending money on legal fees to collect $8. You can assume that a threat to take further action on such small balances is an FDCPA violation.

Review the following criteria to determine if the threat is an empty one:

1. If the balance is small (below $500), the threat is usually an empty one. Few, if any, creditors sue on balances of, for example, $8.
2. If suit is not filed at all, the threat was an empty one. Furthermore, if the suit is not filed shortly after the letter was sent, normally within 30 days, the threat was an empty one.

3. If the letter is sent by a computer, the threat is usually an empty one.

Other false or misleading representations include:

1. stating that if they sell the debt you will lose the right to a defense of non-payment, as in a theft-of-identity situation, where you are not responsible for the debt (Any defense you may have had to the debt carries over to the purchaser of that debt.);
2. telling you that non-payment of the debt is "disgraceful," or that you committed a crime; and
3. reporting false credit information to a credit reporting company.

## FALSE CREDIT INFORMATION

As to the dangers of collection agencies posting reckless and wanton information on the credit report of a consumer, consider the lawsuit of *Rivera v. Bank One*.[13] In this case, the District Court spelled out exactly how debt collectors use credit reports against consumers.

"In the present case," the court stated, "plaintiff (Rivera), a resident of Puerto Rico, is undoubtedly the focus of the activities of which this suit has arisen. The reported account information was included in his credit profile. The mistaken information has allegedly prevented him from purchasing a home in Puerto Rico. The brunt of the harm both in terms of mental anguish suffered by plaintiff and the injury to his credit background was suffered in Puerto Rico. Defendant's conduct was not mere 'untargeted negligence.' Quite to the contrary, a Bank Card issuer's ability to report on the credit habits of its consumers is a powerful tool, designed, in part, to wrench compliance with payment terms from its cardholders. Bank One's alleged refusal to correct mistaken information can only be seen as an attempt to tighten the screws of a non-paying customer."

Collection agencies will report a delinquent debt to the credit reporting bureaus. This is particularly effective on small debts, where the balance is too small to sue over. Once the information goes on the credit report, it will reflect the delinquent status of your account every time you apply for credit. This is a method to coerce you into paying: If you want new credit, the old account must first be paid.

The problem often arises years later, after the debt has been paid off, yet is still listed on the credit report as owing. The collection agency should have corrected the account when it was first paid off, but they didn't bother. While quick to take your money, they're slow to correct the credit report.

In addition to correcting a credit report, however, you may be able to sue the collection agency for falsely reporting the debt as a "current obligation," when, in fact, it was long ago paid off.

Further, the debt collector may not:

1. make false implications that he sold the account to innocent purchasers;
2. claim that he sent you legal documents, or served you, when he didn't;
3. use any other name other than his business's true name;
4. claim that he didn't send you legal process if he did; and,
5. tell you he works for a credit-reporting agency.

Other violations of Section 1692e include sending documents which falsely imply they are approved by the court. For example, a collector cannot send you a summons that has not been legally filed.

Remember, during *every* communication with you, the debt collector must state he is attempting to collect a debt and all information obtained will be used for that purpose. If you are not informed of this, you can sue.

This section also mirrors the fact that you do not have to provide the debt collector with any information about yourself. Unless you're under a court order subpoena, you do not have to tell the debt collector *anything*. He may prompt you. He may say, "I've left 10 messages for you, and you never called back." Or, "Don't you want to pay this bill?" Or, "You weren't home when I called." You don't have to call the collector back. Let him call you. That's his job. He uses the example sentences above to imply that you owe him respect. He owes *you* respect, not visa versa. It's another attempt at "power over."

Another famous line is, "I want your address to confirm your account information." What!? You do *not* give a total stranger, who is trying to take your money, *any* information about yourself! This request is a deceptive ploy to gather yet more information about you.

The use of *any* deceptive means to collect a debt is illegal. The list of prohibited conduct in this section is not final. If conduct that is deceptive occurs, whether listed or not, it is illegal.

# CHAPTER 11

# THE BANKRUPTCY FACTOR

In the majority of all collection cases, debt collection precipitates a bankruptcy. Many consumers have filed bankruptcy simply to escape the debt collector. Even though the consumer may be judgment-proof ("you can't get blood from a stone") people simply cannot deal with the harassment of collectors.

Bankruptcy law and debt collection laws often intertwine. The scope of debt collection must therefore be broken down into three distinct phases:

1. the debt collection occurred *prior* to bankruptcy;
2. the debt collection occurred *during* bankruptcy; and
3. the debt collection occurred *after* bankruptcy.

## PRE-BANKRUPTCY COLLECTION

If the debt collection violation occurred pre-bankruptcy, you can bring an FDCPA lawsuit as long as no bankruptcy is pending. If you bring the lawsuit and *then* file for bankruptcy, your claim is an asset of yours, and becomes the property of the bankruptcy estate. Consult your attorney, as this topic demands more attention than I can give it here. Lawsuits you have pending at the beginning of a bankruptcy—whether the lawsuit is based on collection agency harassment or personal injury—are "owned" by the Bankruptcy Trustee until he decides to keep or abandon them. If you win the lawsuit, the proceeds may go to the Trustee, for distribution to your creditors. Therefore, if possible, attempt to push the pre-bankruptcy lawsuit along, so you obtain a settlement before your bankruptcy filing.

## COLLECTION DURING BANKRUPTCY

If the debt collection violation occurred *during* the bankruptcy, you may not be able to bring a lawsuit in Federal Court. Your sole remedy may be in Bankruptcy Court. During an open bankruptcy, the Bankruptcy Code "preempts," (takes precedence over) the FDCPA. The case *Gray-Mapp v. Sherman,*[14] holds that the bankruptcy discharge injunction (11 U.S.C. 524) preempts the FDCPA. In *Gray-Mapp,* the bankruptcy was open, and the debtor's attorney brought an FDCPA lawsuit in Bankruptcy Court, challenging inflated proofs of claim. A proof of claim is a document a creditor must complete and send to the court in order to receive a distribution of assets, if, indeed, any assets are left for distribution. The bankruptcy was still open when the FDCPA claim was brought in Bankruptcy Court. *Gray-Mapp* held that since the case was still open, the FDCPA claim potentially *interfered* with the administration of the Bankruptcy proceeding, and was therefore preempted by the Bankruptcy Code.

The Bankruptcy Rules provide very adequate protection in the case of any debt collection that occurs during an open bankruptcy. The Automatic

Stay provisions (11 U.S.C. 362) allow you to bring a motion for money damages against a debt collector for collecting debts after the collector knows you filed bankruptcy. If you receive collection calls after you filed bankruptcy, call your lawyer immediately. In addition, tell the collector you filed bankruptcy, and mail them a copy of your bankruptcy notice. Send it certified, return receipt requested.

## POST-BANKRUPTCY COLLECTION

If you receive collection notices *after* bankruptcy, and your case is already closed, then you receive the double protection of both the FDPCA and the discharge injunction of the Bankruptcy Code. Preemption does not seem to apply.

The difference between an open bankruptcy, where the bankruptcy laws do preempt the FDCPA, and a closed bankruptcy, where there is no preemption, is discussed in depth in the case, *Molloy v. Primus Automotive Financial Services*.[15] Basically, it says that the FDCPA rules do not interfere with the administration of a debtor's bankruptcy. And since the FDCPA's purpose is to *prevent* bankruptcy, a debtor whose debt has been discharged is still entitled to the protection of the FDCPA.

In addition to the protection provided by the FDCPA, the bankruptcy laws themselves also offer protection from collection attempts. They state that discharge of a debt in bankruptcy court means that *no* further attempt to collect on that debt is allowed. The law is intentionally broad in scope, because it is intended to prohibit virtually *all* collection efforts.[16]

The legislative history of that section expands on the scope of this injunction: "Subsection 'a' specifies that a discharge in a bankruptcy case voids any judgment and operates as an injunction against the commencement or continuation of an action or any act, including telephone calls, letters, and personal contacts to collect, recover, or offset any discharged debt . . . "[17]

The House and Senate Reports to the Bankruptcy Reform Act of 1978 made clear this intention: "The injunction is to give complete effect to the discharge, and to eliminate any doubt concerning the effect of the discharge as a total prohibition on debt collection efforts. This paragraph has been expanded over a comparable provision in Bankruptcy Act 14f to cover any act to collect, such as dunning by phone or letter . . . "[18] Whether the bankruptcy code preempts the FDCPA or not varies from jurisdiction to jurisdiction. To determine this issue, always consult an attorney in your area.

I stated earlier that debt collectors love to use credit reports to collect debts. If you filed a bankruptcy, and received a discharge, the credit report must reflect that the debt was discharged. The balance must be zero, and the credit report must state, "Discharged in Bankruptcy."

The Fair Credit Reporting Act was recently amended to mandate the accurate reporting of whether the debtor has a Chapter 13 or a Chapter 7 bankruptcy. A Chapter 13 supposedly reflects that you are a better credit risk, because it's considered a "reorganization" rather than a complete liquidation. In a reorganization, the debtor still owes the debt; they just don't owe the whole amount. After a reorganization, the debtor usually owes only pennies on the dollar of the original debt.

Personally, I always thought this emphasis on a 13 being better than a 7 was a scare tactic, to get more consumers to file a 13. In a 13, creditors receive money; in a no-asset 7, they do not. In fact, the bankruptcy amendments being pushed through Congress right now, and promised to be signed into law by President Bush, are merely laws to get more people to file a Chapter 13.

The credit report must reflect whether you filed a Chapter 13 or a Chapter 7. If you filed a 7, the balance of the debts discharged must read, "0—discharged in Bankruptcy." The credit report cannot state, "Charged off for non-payment."

If you have credit reporting errors on your credit report, send a dispute letter to the credit reporting agency, certified, and attached photocopies of documentation to support your position. If the error is not corrected in 30 days, you can actually sue the credit reporting agency. For information on credit reporting agency liability, see *Credit Reporting Fraud: What the Credit Industry Doesn't Want You to Know.*

# CHAPTER 12

# REVIEW COMMUNICATIONS FOR UNFAIR PRACTICES

The list of "unfair practices" is enumerated in Section 1692f. It is not exhaustive. If you believe a practice is unfair, it may very well be. Just because you cannot find the practice in this list, does not mean the practice may not be illegal.

## UNLAWFUL FEES

As stated earlier, collectors usually work on contingency fee agreements with their creditors. For example, a collector may work on a one-third contingency; that is, the collector earns $33.33 for every $100 he collects for his client. When you send the debt collector the $100, the collector deposits the money in a special trust account. He later sends his client a check for $66.67, and keeps $33.33, which is in turn deposited into a general account.

Often a collector will try and collect this contingency fee from *you*. For example, if your debt is $100, you may receive a collection letter for $133.33. If the extra amount does not represent interest and late charges, it may represent the contingency fee, in this case $33.33.

If you receive a letter with a fee tacked on to the balance, you have to ask yourself two questions:

First, did the original contract I signed allow for collection fees?

Second, is the fee reasonable?

The general rule is that if you contracted for "reasonable fees," you may be responsible for paying a fee to the creditor for the collection. Check your original contract. If it states you are liable for costs, attorney fees, and collection fees if the account becomes delinquent, you may very well have to pay these fees.

The analysis, however, does not end there. The second question is, is the fee they want you to pay reasonable? No rule provides an easy answer to this question. You must look at the circumstances. Let's use a one-third fee as an example.

If your debt is $10, and the agency is seeking $13.33, and the contract states they can collect a reasonable fee, I wouldn't complain. It's only $3.33 more than what you owe. But if you owed $10,000, for example, and received a letter stating you owed $13,333.33, I certainly would contact an attorney. The agency is attempting to earn $3,333.33 for sending a single letter, and a court may very well rule that the fee is unreasonable.

However, the chance exists that the fee could "ripen" into a reasonable fee. Let's say you did pay the $13,333.33 after receiving one letter. The collection agency earned a fee of $3,333.33 for sending a single letter, and that is unreasonable. But if the collection efforts get very serious, and perhaps even go to trial on the merits of the case, that $3,333.33 may eventually "ripen" into a reasonable fee through their extended efforts to collect.

The critical point of analysis must focus on whether the collection fee and attorney fees were contracted for. In New York, even interest must be contracted for. If the contract does not allow for the accrual of interest, the collector cannot add interest to the balance due.

## BOUNCED CHECK FEES

Fees for bouncing checks may or may not be allowed, and the court decisions are split on this.

## POST-DATED CHECKS

When a debt collector calls looking for payment, a typical consumer response is, "I don't get paid until next Friday. I'll send you the check then." The debt collector will not let you hang the phone up, and will insist you send him a post-dated check.

Remember I started this book saying the debt collector preys on the "power over" concept? Insisting that you send him a post-dated check is a classic example of this. You can send him one if you want to, but don't let him make you think you *have* to.

Is it legal for a debt collector to ask you for a post-dated check?

Not always!

The post-dated check cannot be post-dated by more than five (5) days, unless the debt collector sends you an agreement in writing to expand the five-day period. Rarely is this rule followed. Collectors *always* accept checks dated much farther than five days away. If they do, a violation of the FDCPA has occurred, and you can sue them. If you sent a post-dated check to a collector, and it is post-dated more than five days with no written agreement, you have a lawsuit against the debt collector. [Appendix I, Section 1692f(2)]

The only exception to this rule is if the collector notifies you, in writing—*not* by phone—of his intent to deposit the check not more than 10 nor less than three (3) business days prior to said deposit. [Appendix I, Section 1692f(3)]. The typical post-dated transaction occurs over the phone, so violations are common.

A debt collector may also not solicit a post-dated check for the purpose of threatening or instituting criminal prosecution. In most states, *intentionally* bouncing a check is a crime. "Intent" may be proved by showing that the check bounced twice. Everyone bounces a check accidentally, at least once in their lives. When a check bounces, the consumer normally runs to the bank and deposits enough money so it won't bounce again. If it does bounce a second time, the courts will often say you intended to bounce it. You may be arrested.

Therefore, a debt collector cannot solicit a post-dated check and then threaten to cash it before the date on the check. This could cause the check to bounce, putting you at legal risk. If you did send him a post-dated check, the debt collector *must* wait until the date on the check before cashing it. He cannot threaten to cash it prior to the date on the check. If he does threaten to do it, or if he actually does it, he violates the FDCPA. [Appendix I, Section 1692f(4)]

## CHARGES AND TELEPHONE FEES

A debt collector cannot call you collect, or make you pay for his special "Telegrams." [Appendix I, Section 1692f(5)] However, if a debt collector makes a deal with you, that he will let you pay less than the full amount of the debt but as a condition the check must be there on a certain day, you may be responsible for overnight charges or mail.

## THREATENING NON-JUDICIAL ACTION

Let's say you have an automobile. A debt collector may not call you up and threaten to take your car away, if the loan is not delinquent. The collector cannot threaten he is going to come by and scoop your furniture up, if it is illegal for him to.

There are two types of loans: secured and unsecured. A good example of an unsecured loan is a credit card. If you default on the credit card payment, the bank has no right to repossess anything, even things you bought with the credit card.

But if you have a secured loan, and don't make a payment on it, the finance company *can* repossess the item.

A secured loan is typically a car loan or a house mortgage, or even a loan used to buy a big item like a television or washer-dryer. If you fail to make a payment on the loan, the bank or finance company has a right to take the property back, because the loan was legally "secured" by the property. The bank will then sell the property at an auction, and you are responsible for the deficiency.

Let's say you have a car worth $5,000, and you owe $8,000 on it. If you don't make payments, the repossession company can take the car and sell it at auction for what they can get. Let's say they get $2,000, and sue you to collect the balance of $6,000 owing on the loan (the $8,000 owed less the $2,000 collected). The remaining $6,000 owed is now unsecured, because the car has already been repossessed.

Virtually every state has a "Right to Cure" law. If you owe $600 on your car, and the repossessor takes the car, it cannot sell the car at auction *until* you have been given the right to redeem it by paying the amount owed. You must be allowed to pay the delinquency and fees and charges and get your car back before it goes to auction.

## CROSS-COLLATERAL CLAUSES

I hate cross-collateral clauses and wish they were all illegal. Usually a consumer has no idea what one is until they have been stung by one.

A cross-collateral clause is when you grant a security interest in not one, but two, pieces of property.

In the example above, I stated that when the car was sold at auction, you still owed $6,000, and that the amount was unsecured because there was nothing else to repossess. In a cross-collateral situation, there is something else to repossess. You granted a security interest in something else.

Suppose you have two cars. One is an older model, and you own it free and clear; the other car is newer, and you owe the bank money on it. The bank will take a cross-collateral on the older car. If you fail to make payments on the new car, the bank has the right to repossess—and sell—*both* of your cars, even though you don't owe money on the older one.

Avoid signing contracts with cross-collateral clauses.

## THE ENVELOPE

The debt collector, except for those legally permissible ways to locate you, cannot legally tell anyone why he is calling you. He cannot share with anyone the fact that you owe a debt, unless he has your permission, or is talking with your spouse, or unless you are a minor and he is talking with your parents. The collector also cannot communicate by postcard, because the collection message is visible. [Appendix I, Section 1692f(7)]

This "right to privacy" is so extreme that it even governs the envelope the debt collector sends the collection letter in. The envelope cannot indicate that it is from a debt collector. The envelope cannot be transparent. No other symbols or lettering other than the return address and "Address Correction Requested" may be on the envelope. A reader or letter carrier should not be able to look at the envelope and tell that a collector sent it.

The name of the collection agency can be allowed on the return address, unless it obviously reflects the fact that it was sent from a collection agency. [Appendix I, Section 1692f(8)]

# LAWSUITS AND DEBT REDUCTION CLINICS

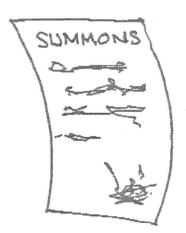

## YOU'VE BEEN SUED

**W**e mentioned earlier that a collector cannot send you official-looking court documents that are not official documents at all. A collector also cannot send you court documents and then try and tell you they are *not* court documents, so you will ignore them and let an important deadline pass.

Let's assume that collection efforts have ripened. The collection agency is tired of your broken promises, and has referred the account to a law firm to get a judgment against you.

First, the law firm is still legally a debt collector, and must abide by the same FDCPA rules and regulations that the collector has to abide by.

The law firm has much more power than a collector. If the law firm wins the lawsuit, they will enter a judgment against you. A judgment is public record, and will absolutely reflect on your credit report. More importantly, it allows the law firm to take judicial measures to collect the debt. Depending on what state you live in, these judicial measures may include: the ability to freeze your bank account, garnish your wages, attach a lien against your house, and even tow your car away.

## THE SUMMONS

The first step the law firm must take is to serve you with a summons. This is usually done with a process server, a person who serves summonses for a living. He or she will knock on your door, hand you the summons, and leave. They will then complete an "Affidavit of Service," stating the date you were served, and including your physical description. This Affidavit is later filed with the Court, and you have a certain number of days to file an answer.

If you've been sued, call a lawyer immediately.

You may someday discover you were never served a summons but still have a judgment against you. Go to the clerk of the court where the judgment is entered and copy your file. You can review the Affidavit of Service, and you may find that the summons was left at an address you never even lived at. *This happens all the time.* Again, take it to your lawyer. Your lawyer can review the Affidavit, and determine if you were properly and lawfully served. If you were not served properly, your lawyer may be able to file a motion with the court to eliminate the judgment against you.

## WHERE YOU WERE SUED

The FDCPA is very particular about where a collector can sue you. Under Section 1692i, you can only be sued a) where you reside; or b) where the contract sued upon was signed. If you are served in an area where you do not reside, or where the contract was not signed, you may actually sue the law firm and debt collector.

For example, if you live in County A, and you went to a hospital located in County B, you can *only* be sued in County A or B. However, if the hospital has a *satellite* branch in County C, and that's where you obtained services, you can only be sued in County A, where you reside, or County C, where the contract for services was signed. Suing you in County B would be a violation of the FDCPA.

These violations are common. A typical scenario is when you live in County A and get services in County A or B, but the company you got services from has its main business offices in County C, and you are sued there, because it's convenient for them. This is not legal.

## ASSET SEARCHES

Skip-tracing companies also do "asset searches," to find out what assets you have. When you pay by check, a copy of your checking account information gets entered into a computer. If a creditor ever wants to find if you have a checking account to freeze (the easiest way to collect a debt), they will look at what banks you previously sent checks in from, and call those banks to determine if the account is still open. If it is, the creditor freezes it.

There are asset search services that offer "blanket restraints." The name and address of every single financial institution in a particular area is fed into a computer owned by the asset search service. If a consumer lives, for example, in Schenectady County, and has a judgment entered against him, the debt collector will use the asset search service to send a restraining order and information subpoena to every bank in Schenectady County, and one other county. (Usually, as a marketing ploy, the debt collector buying the service gets the county the consumer lives in plus one additional county of his choice.) The consumer is quickly located, and his checking accounts frozen.

If that doesn't work, other ploys are used.

As I mentioned before, a debt collector may send a check from a phantom corporation, under the guise that a prize had been won or a refund issued. When the consumer deposits the check, the name of their bank is printed on the back. It's returned to the phantom corporation, and the debt collector just found a bank account to attach.

Or a phantom corporation is designated a "credit bureau," and the debt collector pulls the consumer's credit reports, and does what he pleases with them.

As I said previously, these deceptive acts are violations of the FDCPA, and perhaps the Fair Credit Reporting Act (15 U.S.C. 1681).


## DEBT REDUCTION CLINICS

You'll see companies advertise that they can "reduce your debt." They'll charge you a fee for doing this. Let me say a few words about these companies, and you decide if they're worth it.

Sometimes it truly is better to have an attorney try and negotiate a bill for you, rather than doing it yourself. Generally, you are no match for the credit industry. Your attorney may not be a match for it either, but he or she has a better chance of protecting your rights than you do.

If you're delinquent on your bills, you will find that most credit card companies will offer you a reduced sum automatically. This offer usually arrives when the account is about six months delinquent. The offer is usually for a 40-60% decrease in the amount owed, but the payment must be paid in full, up front.

Why pay a debt reduction clinic, when you may get this decrease yourself?

Some debt reduction clinics will tell you to automatically not pay your bills, and start paying them their "fee" first. Do *not* do this, unless you're filing bankruptcy. The *only* time you should not pay your bills, and only certain bills which your lawyer tells you not to pay, is when you are ready to file bankruptcy. If bankruptcy is not pending, and your credit report looks okay, stay current if possible and try and protect your credit rating.

Be extremely careful of firms that make you pay them instead of your bills. They may claim they are letting money "accumulate" in their account until they can pay the bill in full. But instances exist where you'll never see another dime.

Other companies call themselves "credit counseling services." These companies, many of them well known, advertise that their service is a better alternative than bankruptcy. What they *don't* advertise is that they are owned, manned, and operated by bank and credit officers, who are anxious to keep you paying something on your debt, even though bankruptcy may be a better option that they are willing to tell you. Always consult a bankruptcy lawyer when consulting a credit counseling service.

# CHAPTER 14

# IN-HOUSE
# COLLECTORS

In Chapter 1 I told you that the FDCPA does not apply to creditors acting in their own name. In Chapter 5, I pointed out that collectors working for creditors acting in their own name are called *in-house collectors*. These are employees of the businesses that you actually borrowed the money from, such as banks and credit card companies. These collectors tell you they're calling from their business, and the letters they send you are on their business' letterhead. The FDCPA does *not* apply to collectors who work for the people who extended credit to you. We learned that banks had themselves excluded from the one law designed to protect consumers from the unfair trade practices of collection agencies.

(However, we also learned that if these creditors have a separate collection department that deceptively gives you the impression your account was turned over to a third-party collector, the FDCPA *does* apply.)

If an in-house collector does harass you, you still have several options available. Even though the FDCPA does not apply, other laws protect you. I also know from personal experience that banks and creditors still use the FDCPA as a guideline for their collection departments. Banks have always used the FDCPA as a guideline, but in 1995, the Federal Trade Commission (FTC) actually made it a rule that banks *must* use the FDCPA as a guideline for prohibitions against deceptive and harassing acts and practices.

The FTC has its own rules and regulations prohibiting deceptive acts and practices by banks and collection agencies. Many of these rules mirror the FDCPA, so there is really no use in reproducing them here. If a bank violates the FDCPA and all the rules we went over in this book, there is a good chance it violated the FTC, as well.

The good news is, the FTC regulations are actually much broader than the FDCPA, applying to both creditors acting in their own name and collection agencies.

The bad news is, the FTC rules and regulations offer no *private* cause of action. You read correctly: Even though a bank may violate the FTC regulations, you as an individual cannot sue them for such a violation. *Only the FTC can sue them.*

If a bank, loan company, or any creditor violates the law, you should at least report them to the FTC. If the FTC logs enough complaints against a certain bank or credit card company or auto finance company, the FTC may sue them on their own behalf. You don't necessarily "get your day in court," so to speak, but you can help the government stop the abuser from harassing other people as well.

To file a report with the FTC, you must write them at: The Division of Credit Practices, Federal Trade Commission, Washington, DC, 20580. Or call: (202) 326-3224.

Besides registering your complaint, you have several options available to you in tort. A tort is a "wrongdoing," such as negligence. If you were ever in a car accident, or slipped and fell and sued someone for falling on their property, you sued them for negligence. This is a "tort."

(In collection agency cases, we rarely sue for negligence. We sue for *intentional* violations, such as the Intentional Infliction of Emotional Distress, Harassment, or even Nuisance.)

Each state has different rules regarding these torts, so, as always, consult an attorney. But we must *always* tack a complaint for negligence onto the lawsuit. Why would we do this? There are several reasons.

If the creditor is insured, an insurance company won't pay for "intentional" acts. If the debt collector said something especially rotten to you, or even made a bomb threat, that was a clearly intentional act. You may win the war but lose the battle; that is, you may get a substantial jury verdict but have no pockets to pay you.

So we attach a claim for negligence. First, we may not even prove "intent," and if we don't at least allege negligence, we could lose. Second, the bank itself may argue that their collector was "not acting in the scope of their duty." If an employee is acting in the scope of their duty, they are an *agent* of their employer, and the employer is responsible. But if they are *not* acting in the scope of their duty, then they are not an agent, and therefore the employer—the bank, the credit union, the finance company (the deep pockets, so to speak)—are not responsible for the employee's actions, and will not have to pay an award of damages. If the bank absolutely trained their employees *not* to talk to consumers a certain way, and the employee talks to consumers viciously anyway, the bank may be able to say the employee was not acting in the scope of their employment.

But if you allege negligence, then you can claim the bank was negligent for not supervising and managing the employee properly. Insurance will then apply.

## STATE LAWS

Another option is to consult your attorney and review your state consumer protection laws. Many states have a statute that protects consumers from deceptive acts and practices, and they offer a wide variety of rights and remedies for the aggrieved consumer. The Massachusetts Law 93A, for example, allows the consumer to receive treble (triple) damages. Always review the state law, because it may be even more liberal and wide reaching than laws based in tort.

# CHAPTER 15

# CONCLUSION

We have spent the last umpteen pages reviewing what at first glance appears to be a very easy law to understand. On second look, though, the FDCPA has been interpreted in ways never imagined.

I have had the opportunity to watch several debt collection attorneys give seminars on the FDCPA, and I have never seen one of them tell you what I have told you in this book. They brush over the obvious, such as, "We can't call you at 3 in the morning." They won't tell you things like the fact that they also can't threaten "further action" unless they later sue you. They will gear their seminars to leave you thinking you are at their mercy.

If you go to a bankruptcy lawyer, they will almost always tell you to file bankruptcy. Rarely will a bankruptcy lawyer actually sit down and review why you are there in the first place. Perhaps an unscrupulous car dealer has cheated you in a transaction, and you got mad, didn't pay your bill, and it was repossessed. Perhaps a mortgage company inflated an appraisal, and gave you a loan that was destined to fail from the beginning. *(See Mortgage Fraud: What the Mortgage Industry Doesn't Want You to Know.)* Now you're in foreclosure, and don't know where to turn.

Too many bankruptcy lawyers won't look at the fraud behind the transaction; they will instead assume you simply cannot pay your bills, and will stick you in bankruptcy.

Recently I read that the typical American household can survive something like a month without a paycheck. Imagine. We are all four weeks from homelessness.

People in financial trouble fall into three basic categories. The typical person who calls my office because of collection harassment, for example, is female, between 25 and 45, and is divorced. Women still suffer from a disparity in income from men, and, when they lose the income of their ex-spouse, also suffer a pro rata share in the financial grief that follows a divorce. Financial distress follows every divorce case I have ever seen, and women sadly suffer the brunt of this because they earn less money. In addition, many women have suffered years at the hands of an abuser, and waive their right to equitable distribution and support simply to get rid of the maniac they have been tied to for so long.

The second category is the person who has suffered a traumatic event in their lives: loss of a loved one, an illness, or loss of a job. The plant closes down, and suddenly you have no income.

The last category is the big spenders. Actually, the first two categories deal with why financial distress occurs; this category deals with debt, and may or may not overlap with the other two.

You have heard this statement before, but I will say it again: Americans spend too much and save too little. But before you shrug your shoulders and turn the page, consider something you have not heard before: The spending is not entirely your fault.

We are massaged into being big spenders. If we didn't spend, our economy would collapse. The rest of the world, most of Europe for example, still pays cash for everything, even their houses. My wife has relatives and friends in Europe, and some of them live in spectacular homes. One couple lives in a gigantic mansion made entirely of marble, and he never ever had what we would call a good-paying job. He and his wife lived in a small shack, and built their home one marble brick at a time. Europeans also don't really use credit cards. They pay cash. Germans love to drive their Mercedes Benz. The Mercedes in Germany, however, are stripped models. Germans drive stick shift cars; they don't have automatic transmissions. The cars don't have wiper blades on the headlights (one of the most ridiculous add-ons I have ever seen). They simply cost less because they don't have all the bells and whistles.

Americans demand the bells and whistles because that is how we have come to identify ourselves. We spend more than we earn, so we can drive around in big fancy cars and SUVs we really don't need. When we look at TV commercials advertising all the SUVs, no wonder we want one. Then we receive hundreds of credit card solicitations in the mail, and we're told how much credit we've earned and we feel darn good about ourselves.

My favorite is the "Rent to Own" concept, where you can pay enormous fees for an item like a wide screen television. By the time you have completed the payments, you could have paid cash and had a ton of money left over.

The concept of buying on credit is what keeps our economy going. Our economy is built on stilts. Everyone advertises and tells us how good it is to spend, and how important we are when we spend. Is it any wonder we are trillions of dollars in debt?

Hopefully, you now realize you can fight back. Your financial circumstances may be the result of someone being extremely unscrupulous to you. This book has told you that you do not need to let a collection agent harass you. You don't have to be afraid to pick up your phone and open your mail. Instead, you will be able to read your letters and analyze them and sue the collector if a letter is improper. You will also answer your phone and make a record of all calls and be able to sue the collector if the collector treats you improperly. If you don't want to talk to the collector, you now know you can tell them to simply stop calling you. And if they do contact you, you can sue them.

The collection industry is very big, but is also very greedy. Its members break the laws all the time. Just because its players are large and well financed does not mean they are right and you are wrong. The collection industry is filled with greedy people, and greedy people usually break laws. You can use the knowledge in this book to turn the tables on them. *You* can have power over *them*.

Maybe someday the credit industry will correct its lending practices so the consumer is not destined to lose from the minute the transaction is entered into. Maybe someday the collection industry will run its operations in a lawful way, and teach its players how to respect the consumers they so ruthlessly chase into the ground. Maybe some day auto finance companies will stop charging people 25% interest for a car that will be worth nothing before the loan is paid off, and stop using shady trickery in its selling practices. Maybe someday consumers will stop buying SUVs and identifying themselves with what they drive rather than who they are.

Maybe someday the cow will jump over the moon.

# FAIR DEBT COLLECTION PRACTICES ACT (FDCPA)– U.S. CODE 15

## Section 1692. Congressional findings and declaration of purpose

• **(a) Abusive practices**

There is abundant evidence of the use of abusive, deceptive, and unfair debt collection practices by many debt collectors. Abusive debt collection practices contribute to the number of personal bankruptcies, to marital instability, to the loss of jobs, and to invasions of individual privacy.

• **(b) Inadequacy of laws**

Existing laws and procedures for redressing these injuries are inadequate to protect consumers.

• **(c) Available non-abusive collection methods**

Means other than misrepresentation or other abusive debt collection practices are available for the effective collection of debts.

• **(d) Interstate commerce**

Abusive debt collection practices are carried on to a substantial extent in interstate commerce and through means and instrumentalities of such commerce. Even where abusive debt collection practices are purely intrastate in character, they nevertheless directly affect interstate commerce.

• **(e) Purposes**

It is the purpose of this subchapter to eliminate abusive debt collection practices by debt collectors, to insure that those debt collectors who refrain from using abusive debt collection practices are not competitively disadvantaged, and to promote consistent State action to protect consumers against debt collection abuses.

## Sec. 1692a. Definitions

As used in this subchapter—

- **(1)** The term "Commission" means the Federal Trade Commission.
- **(2)** The term "communication" means the conveying of information regarding a debt directly or indirectly to any person through any medium.
- **(3)** The term "consumer" means any natural person obligated or allegedly obligated to pay any debt.
- **(4)** The term "creditor" means any person who offers or extends credit creating a debt or to whom a debt is owed, but such term does not include any person to the extent that he receives an assignment or transfer of a debt in default solely for the purpose of facilitating collection of such debt for another.
- **(5)** The term "debt" means any obligation or alleged obligation of a consumer to pay money arising out of a transaction in which the money, property, insurance, or services which are the subject of the transaction are primarily for personal, family, or household purposes, whether or not such obligation has been reduced to judgment.
- **(6)** The term "debt collector" means any person who uses any instrumentality of interstate commerce or the mails in any business the principal purpose of which is the collection of any debts, or who regularly collects or attempts to collect, directly or indirectly, debts owed or due or asserted to be owed or due another. Notwithstanding the exclusion provided by clause (F) of the last sentence of this paragraph, the term includes any creditor who, in the process of collecting his own debts, uses any name other than his own which would indicate that a third person is collecting or attempting to collect such debts. For the purpose of section 1692f(6) of this title, such term also includes any person who uses any instrumentality of interstate commerce or the mails in any business the principal purpose of which is the enforcement of security interests. The term does not include—
  - **(A)** any officer or employee of a creditor while, in the name of the creditor, collecting debts for such creditor;
  - **(B)** any person while acting as a debt collector for another person, both of whom are related by common ownership or affiliated by corporate control,

if the person acting as a debt collector does so only for persons to whom it is so related or affiliated and if the principal business of such person is not the collection of debts;

- **(C)** any officer or employee of the United States or any State to the extent that collecting or attempting to collect any debt is in the performance of his official duties;

- **(D)** any person while serving or attempting to serve legal process on any other person in connection with the judicial enforcement of any debt;

- **(E)** any nonprofit organization which, at the request of consumers, performs bona fide consumer credit counseling and assists consumers in the liquidation of their debts by receiving payments from such consumers and distributing such amounts to creditors; and

- **(F)** any person collecting or attempting to collect any debt owed or due or asserted to be owed or due another to the extent such activity (i) is incidental to a bona fide fiduciary obligation or a bona fide escrow arrangement; (ii) concerns a debt which was originated by such person; (iii) concerns a debt which was not in default at the time it was obtained by such person; or (iv) concerns a debt obtained by such person as a secured party in a commercial credit transaction involving the creditor.

- **(7)** The term "location information" means a consumer's place of abode and his telephone number at such place, or his place of employment.

- **(8)** The term "State" means any State, territory, or possession of the United States, the District of Columbia, the Commonwealth of Puerto Rico, or any political subdivision of any of the foregoing.

## Sec. 1692b. Acquisition of location information

Any debt collector communicating with any person other than the consumer for the purpose of acquiring location information about the consumer shall—

- **(1)** identify himself, state that he is confirming or correcting location information concerning the consumer, and, only if expressly requested, identify his employer;

- **(2)** not state that such consumer owes any debt;

- **(3)** not communicate with any such person more than once unless requested to do so by such person or unless the debt collector reasonably believes that the earlier response of such person is erroneous or incomplete and that such person now has correct or complete location information;

- **(4)** not communicate by post card;

- **(5)** not use any language or symbol on any envelope or in the contents of any communication effected by the mails or telegram that indicates that the debt collector is in the debt collection business or that the communication relates to the collection of a debt; and

- **(6)** after the debt collector knows the consumer is represented by an attorney with regard to the subject debt and has knowledge of, or can readily ascertain, such attorney's name and address, not communicate with any person other than that attorney, unless the attorney fails to respond within a reasonable period of time to communication from the debt collector.

## Sec. 1692c. Communication in connection with debt collection

- **(a) Communication with the consumer generally**

Without the prior consent of the consumer given directly to the debt collector or the express permission of a court of competent jurisdiction, a debt collector may not communicate with a consumer in connection with the collection of any debt—

- **(1)** at any unusual time or place or a time or place known or which should be known to be inconvenient to the consumer. In the absence of knowledge of circumstances to the contrary, a debt collector shall assume that the convenient time for communicating with a consumer is after 8 o'clock antemeridian and before 9 o'clock postmeridian, local time at the consumer's location;

- **(2)** if the debt collector knows the consumer is represented by an attorney with respect to such debt and has knowledge of, or can readily ascertain, such attorney's name and address, unless the attorney fails to respond within a reasonable period of time to a communication from the debt collector or unless the attorney consents to direct communication with the consumer; or

- **(3)** at the consumer's place of employment if the debt collector knows or has reason to know that the consumer's employer prohibits the consumer from receiving such communication.

- **(b) Communication with third parties**

Except as provided in section 1692b of this title, without the prior consent of the consumer given directly to the debt collector, or the express permission of a court of competent jurisdiction, or as reasonably necessary to effectuate a postjudgment judicial remedy, a debt collector may not communicate, in connection with the collection of any debt, with any person other than the consumer, his attorney, a consumer reporting agency if otherwise permitted by law, the creditor, the attorney of the creditor, or the attorney of the debt collector.

- **(c) Ceasing communication**

If a consumer notifies a debt collector in writing that the consumer refuses to pay a debt or that the consumer wishes the debt collector to cease further communication with the consumer, the debt collector shall not communicate further with the consumer with respect to such debt, except—

- **(1)** to advise the consumer that the debt collector's further efforts are being terminated;

- **(2)** to notify the consumer that the debt collector or creditor may invoke specified remedies which are ordinarily invoked by such debt collector or creditor; or

- **(3)** where applicable, to notify the consumer that the debt collector or creditor intends to invoke a specified remedy. If such notice from the consumer is made by mail, notification shall be complete upon receipt.

- **(d) "Consumer" defined**

For the purpose of this section, the term "consumer" includes the consumer's spouse, parent (if the consumer is a minor), guardian, executor, or administrator.

## Sec. 1692d. Harassment or abuse

A debt collector may not engage in any conduct the natural consequence of which is to harass, oppress, or abuse any person in connection with the collection of a debt. Without limiting the general application of the foregoing, the following conduct is a violation of this section:

- **(1)** The use or threat of use of violence or other criminal means to harm the physical person, reputation, or property of any person.
- **(2)** The use of obscene or profane language or language the natural consequence of which is to abuse the hearer or reader.
- **(3)** The publication of a list of consumers who allegedly refuse to pay debts, except to a consumer reporting agency or to persons meeting the requirements of section 1681a(f) or 1681b(3) [1] of this title.
- **(4)** The advertisement for sale of any debt to coerce payment of the debt.
- **(5)** Causing a telephone to ring or engaging any person in telephone conversation repeatedly or continuously with intent to annoy, abuse, or harass any person at the called number.
- **(6)** Except as provided in section 1692b of this title, the placement of telephone calls without meaningful disclosure of the caller's identity.

## Sec. 1692e. False or misleading representations

A debt collector may not use any false, deceptive, or misleading representation or means in connection with the collection of any debt. Without limiting the general application of the foregoing, the following conduct is a violation of this section:

- **(1)** The false representation or implication that the debt collector is vouched for, bonded by, or affiliated with the United States or any State, including the use of any badge, uniform, or facsimile thereof.
- **(2)** The false representation of—
  - **(A)** the character, amount, or legal status of any debt; or
  - **(B)** any services rendered or compensation which may be lawfully received by any debt collector for the collection of a debt.

- **(3)** The false representation or implication that any individual is an attorney or that any communication is from an attorney.
- **(4)** The representation or implication that nonpayment of any debt will result in the arrest or imprisonment of any person or the seizure, garnishment, attachment, or sale of any property or wages of any person unless such action is lawful and the debt collector or creditor intends to take such action.
- **(5)** The threat to take any action that cannot legally be taken or that is not intended to be taken.
- **(6)** The false representation or implication that a sale, referral, or other transfer of any interest in a debt shall cause the consumer to—
  - **(A)** lose any claim or defense to payment of the debt; or
  - **(B)** become subject to any practice prohibited by this subchapter.
- **(7)** The false representation or implication that the consumer committed any crime or other conduct in order to disgrace the consumer.
- **(8)** Communicating or threatening to communicate to any person credit information which is known or which should be known to be false, including the failure to communicate that a disputed debt is disputed.
- **(9)** The use or distribution of any written communication which simulates or is falsely represented to be a document authorized, issued, or approved by any court, official, or agency of the United States or any State, or which creates a false impression as to its source, authorization, or approval.
- **(10)** The use of any false representation or deceptive means to collect or attempt to collect any debt or to obtain information concerning a consumer.
- **(11)** The failure to disclose in the initial written communication with the consumer and, in addition, if the initial communication with the consumer is oral, in that initial oral communication, that the debt collector is attempting to collect a debt and that any information obtained will be used for that purpose, and the failure to disclose in subsequent communications that the communication is from a debt collector, except that this paragraph shall not apply to a formal pleading made in connection with a legal action.

- **(12)** The false representation or implication that accounts have been turned over to innocent purchasers for value.
- **(13)** The false representation or implication that documents are legal process.
- **(14)** The use of any business, company, or organization name other than the true name of the debt collector's business, company, or organization.
- **(15)** The false representation or implication that documents are not legal process forms or do not require action by the consumer.
- **(16)** The false representation or implication that a debt collector operates or is employed by a consumer reporting agency as defined by section 1681a(f) of this title.

## Sec. 1692f. Unfair Practices

A debt collector may not use unfair or unscrupulous means to collect or attempt to collect a debt. Following are examples of conduct that apply to unfair practice violations.

- **(1)** The collection of any amount of interest, fee charge, or other expense related to the debt unless specifically authorized by the original debt agreement or permitted by law.
- **(2)** The accepting of any check by the debt collector postdated by more than five days is not legal, unless the debt collector notifies the person in writing of their intent to deposit the check not more than ten nor less than three business days prior to the deposit.
- **(3)** A debt collector asking for a postdated check or any other postdated payment for the purpose of threatening or starting criminal prosecution.
- **(4)** Depositing or threatening to deposit a postdated check or other postdated payment before the written date.
- **(5)** Charging for communications by concealing the true reason for the communication. Examples of this are: collect telephone calls and telegram fees.
- **(6)** Taking or threatening to take any nonjudicial action to effect dispossession or disablement of property if—

- **(A)** there is no present right to possession of the property claimed as collateral through an enforceable security interest;
- **(B)** there is no present intention to take possession of the property; or
- **(C)** the property is exempt by law from dispossession or disablement.
- **(7)** Communicating with a consumer regarding a debt by postcard.
- **(8)** Using any language or symbol, other than the debt collector's address, on any envelope when communicating with a consumer by use of the mails or by telegram, except that a debt collector may use his business name if such name does not indicate that he is in the debt collection business.

## Sec. 1692g. Validation of debts

- **(a) Notice of debt; contents**

Within five days after the initial communication with a consumer in connection with the collection of any debt, a debt collector shall, unless the following information is contained in the initial communication or the consumer has paid the debt, send the consumer a written notice containing—

- **(1)** the amount of the debt;
- **(2)** the name of the creditor to whom the debt is owed;
- **(3)** a statement that unless the consumer, within thirty days after receipt of the notice, disputes the validity of the debt, or any portion thereof, the debt will be assumed to be valid by the debt collector;
- **(4)** a statement that if the consumer notifies the debt collector in writing within the thirty-day period that the debt, or any portion thereof, is disputed, the debt collector will obtain verification of the debt or a copy of a judgment against the consumer and a copy of such verification or judgment will be mailed to the consumer by the debt collector; and
- **(5)** a statement that, upon the consumer's written request within the thirty-day period, the debt collector will provide the consumer with the name and address of the original creditor, if different from the current creditor.

- **(b) Disputed debts**

If the consumer notifies the debt collector in writing within the thirty-day period described in subsection (a) of this section that the debt, or any portion thereof, is disputed, or that the consumer requests the name and address of the original creditor, the debt collector shall cease collection of the debt, or any disputed portion thereof, until the debt collector obtains verification of the debt or a copy of a judgment, or the name and address of the original creditor, and a copy of such verification or judgment, or name and address of the original creditor, is mailed to the consumer by the debt collector.

- **(c) Admission of liability**

The failure of a consumer to dispute the validity of a debt under this section may not be construed by any court as an admission of liability by the consumer.

## Sec. 1692h. Multiple debts

If any consumer owes multiple debts and makes any single payment to any debt collector with respect to such debts, such debt collector may not apply such payment to any debt which is disputed by the consumer and, where applicable, shall apply such payment in accordance with the consumer's directions.

## Sec. 1692i. Legal actions by debt collectors

- **(a) Venue**

Any debt collector who brings any legal action on a debt against any consumer shall—

- **(1)** in the case of an action to enforce an interest in real property securing the consumer's obligation, bring such action only in a judicial district or similar legal entity in which such real property is located; or

- **(2)** in the case of an action not described in paragraph (1), bring such action only in the judicial district or similar legal entity—

  - **(A)** in which such consumer signed the contract sued upon; or

  - **(B)** in which such consumer resides at the commencement of the action.

- **(b) Authorization of actions**

Nothing in this subchapter shall be construed to authorize the bringing of legal actions by debt collectors.

## Sec. 1692j. Furnishing certain deceptive forms

- **(a)** It is unlawful to design, compile, and furnish any form knowing that such form would be used to create the false belief in a consumer that a person other than the creditor of such consumer is participating in the collection of or in an attempt to collect a debt such consumer allegedly owes such creditor, when in fact such person is not so participating.

- **(b)** Any person who violates this section shall be liable to the same extent and in the same manner as a debt collector is liable under section 1692k of this title for failure to comply with a provision of this subchapter.

## Sec. 1692k. Civil liability

- **(a) Amount of damages**

Except as otherwise provided by this section, any debt collector who fails to comply with any provision of this subchapter with respect to any person is liable to such person in an amount equal to the sum of—

- **(1)** any actual damage sustained by such person as a result of such failure;

- **(2)**

  - **(A)** in the case of any action by an individual, such additional damages as the court may allow, but not exceeding $1,000; or

  - **(B)** in the case of a class action, (i) such amount for each named plaintiff as could be recovered under subparagraph (A), and

    (ii) such amount as the court may allow for all other class members, without regard to a minimum individual recovery, not to exceed the lesser of $500,000 or 1 per centum of the net worth of the debt collector; and

- **(3)** in the case of any successful action to enforce the foregoing liability, the costs of the action, together with a reasonable attorney's fee as determined by the court. On a finding by the court that an action under this section was brought in bad faith and for the purpose of harassment, the court may award to the defendant attorney's fees reasonable in relation to the work expended and costs.

- **(b) Factors considered by court**
In determining the amount of liability in any action under subsection (a) of this section, the court shall consider, among other relevant factors—

- **(1)** in any individual action under subsection (a)(2)(A) of this section, the frequency and persistence of noncompliance by the debt collector, the nature of such noncompliance, and the extent to which such noncompliance was intentional; or

- **(2)** in any class action under subsection (a)(2)(B) of this section, the frequency and persistence of noncompliance by the debt collector, the nature of such noncompliance, the resources of the debt collector, the number of persons adversely affected, and the extent to which the debt collector's noncompliance was intentional.

- **(c) Intent**
A debt collector may not be held liable in any action brought under this subchapter if the debt collector shows by a preponderance of evidence that the violation was not intentional and resulted from a bona fide error notwithstanding the maintenance of procedures reasonably adapted to avoid any such error.

- **(d) Jurisdiction**
An action to enforce any liability created by this subchapter may be brought in any appropriate United States district court without regard to the amount in controversy, or in any other court of competent jurisdiction, within one year from the date on which the violation occurs.

- **(e) Advisory opinions of Commission**
No provision of this section imposing any liability shall apply to any act done or omitted in good faith in conformity with any advisory opinion of the Commission,

notwithstanding that after such act or omission has occurred, such opinion is amended, rescinded, or determined by judicial or other authority to be invalid for any reason.

## SAMPLES OF LEGAL COMPLAINTS

### SAMPLE #1
### Failure to provide right to dispute language 1692g

UNITED STATES DISTRICT COURT
DISTRICT OF

_____

YOU,

                    Plaintiff,

      -against-

THEM Collections,

                    Defendants,

_____

COMPLAINT

JURY DEMAND

Index No.

1. Plaintiff, YOU, brings this action for redress of Defendants' violations of the Fair Debt Collection Practices Act, 15 U.S.C. 1692 et. seq (hereinafter "FDCPA").

### JURISDICTION

2. Jurisdiction is vested in this Court pursuant to 15 U.S.C. 1692k(d) and 28 U.S.C. 1337.

### PARTIES

3. Plaintiff, YOU, is a natural person residing at Anywhere Ave., Anywhere, New York.

4. The defendant, THEM collections, is a debt collector, and maintains a place of business at Elsewhere, Connecticut.

## FACTUAL ALLEGATIONS

5. On or about November 13, 2000, defendants mailed plaintiff a letter for the collection of consumer debt. A true and just copy of this letter is attached hereto as Exhibit "A".

6. The letter fails to comply with the Fair Debt Collection Practices Act ("FDCPA"), 15 U.S.C. 1692 et. seq.

7. The letter in Exhibit "A" fails to state to the consumer that unless the consumer, within thirty days after receipt of the notice, disputes the validity of the debt, or any portion thereof, the debt will be assumed to be valid by the debt collector, in violation of 15 U.S.C. 1692g and e(10).

8. The letter in Exhibit "A" fails to provide the statement that if the consumer notifies the debt collector in writing within the thirty day period that the debt, or an portion thereof, is disputed, the debt collector will obtain verification of the debt or a copy of a judgment against the consumer and a copy of such verification or judgment will be mailed to the consumer and e(10).

9. The letter in Exhibit "A" fails to provide a statement that, upon the consumers written request within the thirty day period, the debt collector will provide the consumer with the name and address of the original creditor, if different from the current creditor, in violation of 15 U.S.C. 1692g and e(10).

10. The letter in Exhibit "A" fails to notify the consumer that if the consumer notifies the debt collector in writing within the thirty day period described in subsection (a) of this section that the debt, or any portion thereof, is disputed, or that the consumer requests the name and address of the original creditor, the debt collector shall cease collection of the debt, or any disputed portion thereof, until the debt collector obtains verification of the debt or a copy of a judgment, or the name and address of the original creditor, and a copy of such verification or judgment, or name and address of the original creditor, is mailed to the consumer by the debt collector in violation of 15 U.S.C. 1692g.

## COUNT I
### 15 U.S.C. 1692g

11. Plaintiff repeats and re-alleges the allegations in paragraphs 1-10 as if fully set forth herein.

12. Defendants violated 15 U.S.C. 1692g as to plaintiff by failing to use the language mandated by 15 U.S.C. 1692g.

13. As a result of defendant's violations of the FDCPA, plaintiff is entitled to recover statutory damages pursuant to 15 U.S.C. 1692k.

WHEREFORE, as to Count I, plaintiff respectfully requests that judgment be entered in her favor and against defendants for:

(a) Statutory damages pursuant to 15 U.S.C. 1692k;

(b) Costs and reasonable attorney fees pursuant to 15 U.S.C. 1692k;

(c) A right to a trial by jury;

(d) For such other and further relief as to this Court seems just and proper.

Respectfully submitted,

RICHARD L. DIMAGGIO
Attorney for plaintiff
P.O. Box 104
Clifton Park, New York 12065

## SAMPLE #2
### Contacting at Work, Harassment

UNITED STATES DISTRICT COURT
DISTRICT OF
_____

YOU,
                    Plaintiff,
                                              Index No.
          -against-
                                              JURY DEMAND
THEM collections,                             COMPLAINT
                    Defendant.
_____

1. Plaintiff, YOU, brings this action for redress of Defendants violations of the Fair Debt Collection Practices Act, 15 U.S.C. 1692 et. seq. (hereinafter "FDCPA"). Defendants, by and through their employees and supervisors, repeatedly contacted plaintiff at work, when she asked them not to.

### JURISDICTION

2. Jurisdiction is vested in this Court pursuant to 15 U.S.C. 1692k(d) and 28 U.S.C. 1337.

### PARTIES

3. Plaintiff, YOU, is a natural person residing at Anywhere Ave., Anywhere, Maryland.

4. The defendant, THEM Collections, is a domestic corporation and a debt collector, and maintains a place of business at Anywhere, Va.

### FACTUAL ALLEGATIONS

5. This case arises out of non-payment of a credit card in plaintiff's name, to wit, a BBBB Bank card, account number 1234567, with a balance of $2,663.81.

6. That this account went into collections is not in dispute; the account was referred to Defendants herein for collections.

7. Defendants, specifically a collector named or identified as "Rich Davis"—perhaps a desk name—called plaintiff many times at work. Plaintiff repeatedly told Davis not to call her at work, that work is an inconvenient time to be contacted.

8. Despite the information, Davis called plaintiff repeatedly at work at her place of employment, XYZ Corporation.

9. During the conversations, Davis told plaintiff that if she didn't pay the bill by 4 o'clock that afternoon, he would sue her.

10. Plaintiff told Davis if he continued to harass her at work, she would get a lawyer. Davis told her, "I know enough about the law to be a lawyer myself. I'll talk to your lawyer. I'll chew him out. He's just somebody that went to school a year longer than you and me."

11. Plaintiff told Davis she could not receive calls at work because she was a nurse and took care of patients. Davis told plaintiff, "You don't take care of patients with a two year degree. What kind of degree do you have anyway?"

12. Plaintiff said again, "I asked you not to call me at work." Davis responded, "And I told you to send me a payment."

13. Davis also discovered plaintiff lived in a mobile home. He told plaintiff, "I don't have to deal with your type up in that trailer."

14. Davis told plaintiff that if she did not pay "I'll send the sheriff to your place of employment and he'll arrest you."

## COUNT I
### 15 U.S.C. 1692 et. seq.
### 1692c(a)(1), 1692c(a)(3), 1692c(b), 1692c(c), 1692 d, 1692e

15. Plaintiff repeats and reiterates allegations in paragraphs 1-14 above, as if fully set forth herein.

16. Contacting plaintiff at work, at a place where the collector knows is inconvenient, is a violation of 1692c.

17. Contacting plaintiff at work, at a place where the collector knows is inconvenient, and where the collector knows that the employer prohibits such communication, is a violation of 1692c(a)(3).

18. Contacting plaintiff after being requested not to is a violation of 1692c(c).

19. Causing the phone to ring repeatedly and continuously, with intent to annoy, abuse and harass plaintiff is a violation of 1692d(5).

20. The facts herein alleged constitute a false and misleading attempt to collect a debt, in violation of 1692e.

21. The facts herein alleged constitute an unfair practice, and is in violation of 1692f.

22. The facts herein constitute acts of harassment and abuse, in violation of 15 U.S.C. 1692d.

23. The facts herein, including but not limited to the threat of arrest, constitute a violation of 15 U.S.C. 1692e.

24. The facts herein, including but not limited to the threat of arrest, constitute a violation of 15 U.S.C. 1692e, e(7), e(4) and e(5).

25. The facts herein, including the statements that Davis "knows as much as any lawyer" is false and misleading and is a violation of 15 U.S.C. 1692e(3).

26. That all said acts were done intentionally, willfully and maliciously.

27. That the plaintiff herein suffered emoitonal distress, anxiety and hu-miliation and is entitled to punitive damages and actual damages.

WHEREFORE, as to Count I, plaintiffs respectfully requests that judgment be entered in their favor and against defendants for:

(a) Statutory damages pursuant to 15 U.S.C. 1692k;

(b) Costs and reasonable attorney fees pursuant to 15 U.S.C. 1692k;

(c) A right to a trial by jury;

(d) For such other and further relief as to this Court seems just and proper.

Respectfully submitted,

RICHARD L. DIMAGGIO
Attorney for plaintiff
P.O. Box 104
Clifton Park, New York 12065

**SAMPLE #3**
Class Action
Threat of "Further Action"

UNITED STATES DISTRICT COURT
DISTRICT OF

_____

YOU, individually and on behalf
of all others similarly situated,

<table>
<tr><td>Plaintiff,</td><td>COMPLAINT</td></tr>
<tr><td>-against-</td><td>JURY DEMAND</td></tr>
</table>

THEM SERVICE AGENCY, and

<table>
<tr><td>Defendant</td><td>Index No.</td></tr>
</table>

"C. BASS"

Defendants,

_____

## CLASS ACTION COMPLAINT

1. Plaintiff, YOU, individually and on behalf of all others similarly situated, brings this action for redress of Defendants' violations of the Fair Debt Collection Practices Act, 15 U.S.C. 1692 et. seq. (hereinafter "FDCPA").

### JURISDICTION

2. Jurisdiction is vested in this Court pursuant to 15 U.S.C. 1692k(d) and 28 U.S.C. 1337.

### PARTIES

3. Plaintiff, YOU ("You"), is a natural person residing at 8C Village, Anywhere, Springfield, MA.

4. The defendant, THEM SERVICE AGENCY ("Them"), is a debt collector, and maintains a place of business in Anywhere, TX.

5. The defendant, C. BASS ("Bass"), is a debt collector, is the owner and CEO of THEM, drafted the letter which is the subject matter of this litigation (Exhibit "A", attached hereto), and maintains his business in Anywhere, TX.

FACTUAL ALLEGATIONS

6. On or about July 21, 1999, defendants mailed plaintiff a letter for the collection of consumer debt. A true and just copy of this letter is attached hereto as Exhibit "A"

7. The letter fails to comply with the Fair Debt Collection Practices Act ("FDCPA"), 15 U.S.C. 1692 et. seq.

8. The letter states, in part, that payment must be made within ten days to avoid "possible" legal action, and said language overrides the thirty (30) day right to dispute, in violation of 15 U.S.C. 1692e(5) and (10), and 15 U.S.C. 1692g.

9. The letter in Exhibit "A" fails to state to the consumer that unless the consumer, within thirty days after receipt of the notice, disputes the validity of the debt, or any portion thereof, the debt will be assumed to be valid by the debt collector, in violation of 15 U.S.C. 1692g and e(10).

10. The letter in Exhibit "A" fails to provide the statement that if the consumer notifies the debt collector in writing within the thirty day period that the debt, or an portion thereof, is disputed, the debt collector will obtain verification of the debt or a copy of a judgment against the consumer and a copy of such verification or judgment will be mailed to the consumer by the debt collector, in violation of 15 U.S.C. 1692g and e(10).

11. The letter in Exhibit "A" fails to provide a statement that, upon the consumer's written request within the thirty day period, the debt collector will provide the consumer with the name and address of the original creditor, if different from the current creditor, in violation of 15 U.S.C. 1692g and e(10).

12. The letter in Exhibit "A" fails to notify the consumer that if the consumer notifies the debt collector in writing within the thirty day period described in subsection (a) of this section that the debt, or any portion thereof, is disputed, or that the consumer requests the name and address of the original creditor, the debt

collector shall cease collection of the debt, or any disputed portion thereof, until the debt collector obtains verification of the debt or a copy of a judgment, or the name and address of the original creditor, and a copy of such verification or judgment, or name and address of the original creditor, is mailed to the consumer by the debt collector in violation of 15 U.S.C. 1692g and e(10).

## COUNT I – CLASS ALLEGATIONS

13. Plaintiff repeats and reiterates allegations in paragraphs 1-12 above, as if fully set forth herein.

14. This claim is brought on behalf of a class. The class consists of all persons who satisfy the following criteria:

a. They received a form letter from defendants similar to Exhibit "A";

b. The transaction from which the alleged debt arose was for personal, family or household purposes;

c. The letter was sent within one year prior to the date of the filing of this action.

15. There are common questions of law or fact which predominate over individual questions peculiar to individual class members. The predominate common question is whether defendant's use of the form letter violates the FDCPA.

16. Plaintiff's claims are typical of those of the class. All are based on the same legal and factual theories.

17. Plaintiff will fairly and adequately represent the interests of the class members. Neither plaintiff nor her counsel have any interests which might cause them not to vigorously pursue this action. Plaintiff's counsel is experienced in handling class action litigation pursuant to the Fair Debt Collection Practices Act.

18. A class action is superior for the fair and efficient adjudication of this controversy. Most class members do not realize they have a claim. A class action is therefore essential to prevent a failure of justice. Furthermore, even if a class member did realize that he or she had a claim, the size of the claims involved does not warrant individual litigation of the necessary magnitude and complexity.

19. Defendants violated 15 U.S.C. 1692g as to plaintiff and each member of the class failing to use the language mandated by 15 U.S.C. 1692g.

20. Defendants violated 15 U.S.C. 1692e(10) as to plaintiff and each member of the class by not using the language mandated by 15 U.S.C. 1692g, and notifying consumers of their rights.

21. Defendants violated 15 U.S.C. 1692e and e(10) as to plaintiff and as to each member of the class, by using the false representations and deceptive means with the collection of alleged debts.

22. Defendants violated 15 U.S.C. 1692g, by demanding payment, and said demand for payment conflicts with the thirty (30) day right to dispute.

23. As a result of defendants violations of the FDCPA, plaintiff and members of the class are entitled to recover statutory damages pursuant to 15 U.S.C. 1692k(a)(2).

WHEREFORE, as to Count I, plaintiff respectfully requests that judgment be entered in her favor of the class and against defendants for:

(a) Statutory damages pursuant to 15 U.S.C. 1692k;

(b) Costs and reasonable attorney fees pursuant to 15 U.S.C. 1692k;

(c) A right to class certification;

(d) A right to a trial by jury;

(e) For such other and further relief as to this Court seems just and proper.

Respectfully submitted,

RICHARD L. DIMAGGIO
Attorney for plaintiff
P.O. Box 104
Clifton Park, New York 12065

## SAMPLE #4

### Collection on Time-Barred Debt
### False Items on Collection Report
### Post-Dated (Electronic) Check Held More Than 5 Days

UNITED STATES DISTRICT COURT
DISTRICT OF

---

YOU,

                  Plaintiff,

      -against-

THEM SYSTEMS,

                 Defendant.

COMPLAINT

JURY DEMAND

Index No.

---

1. Plaintiffs, YOU, brings this action for redress of Defendants violations of the Fair Debt Collection Practices Act, 15 U.S.C. 1692 et. seq. (hereinafter "FDCPA"), based on 1) attempting to collect on a time barred debt against both parties, where the statute of limitations to sue on the debt has passed years ago in violation of 15 U.S.C. 1692e(2)(A), 15 U.S.C. 1692e(5), 15 U.S.C. 1692e(10); 2) threatening to take action that cannot be legally taken, namely, threatening to place derogatory remarks on a credit report regarding information which exceeds limitations of the Fair Credit Reporting Act requirement (15 U.S.C. 1681 et. seq.), all in violation of 15 U.S.C. 1692e(2)(A), 15 U.S.C. 1692e(5), 15 U.S.C. 1692e(10); and 3) holding funds and a post dated check for more than five days, in violation of 1692f(2).

### JURISDICTION

2. Jurisdiction is vested in this Court pursuant to 15 U.S.C. 1692k(d) and 28 U.S.C. 1337.

## PARTIES

3. Plaintiff, YOU, is a natural person residing at South Street, Anywhere, NY.

4. The defendant, THEM SYSTEMS ("Them") is a debt collector, and maintains a place of business in, Austin, TX.

## FACTUAL ALLEGATIONS

5. Plaintiff YOU filed Ch. 7 bankruptcy in 1996, and your debts were discharged (Case No. 11-11111).

6. Included in that discharge was a Bank card with a balance of approximately $1,271 dollars.

7. The Bank card was last used and active sometime in the late 1980s.

8. The Statute of Limitations to sue on a debt in New York State based on contract is 6 years.

9. Upon information and belief, at some point in time defendant herein purchased plaintiff's debt for cents on the dollar for the purpose of collection.

10. Defendants called Plaintiff at work and said, "So what are you going to do about this debt incurred a year ago?"

11. Defendants also told him, "We want this resolved by noon on Friday, or we will put it on your credit report."

12. Defendants demanded money from plaintiff, indicated continuing efforts to collect on the debt, and proceeded to accept an electronic payment from plaintiff. The electronic payment was in the form of an electronic "check" which defendants told plaintiff they would hold for more than five days.

13. At no time did defendants tell Plaintiff they could not otherwise collect on the debt or that he did not have to reaffirm the debt.

## COUNT I
### 15 U.S.C. 1692e(2)(A), e(5), e(10)

14. Plaintiff repeats and reiterates allegations in paragraphs 1-13 above, as if fully set forth herein.

15. Attempting to collect on a time barred debt against both parties, where the statute of limitations to sue on the debt has passed years ago is a violation of 15 U.S.C. 1692e(2)(A), as it misrepresents the character and amount of the debt.

16. Attempting to collect on a time barred debt against both parties, where the statute of limitations to sue on the debt has passed years ago is a violation of 15 U.S.C. 1692e(5), as it is a threat to take any action that cannot legally be taken.

17. Attempting to collect on a time barred debt against both parties, where the statute of limitations to sue on the debt has passed years ago is a violation of 15 U.S.C. 1692e(10), as it is the use of a false and deceptive means to attempt to collect a debt.

WHEREFORE, as to Count I, plaintiffs respectfully requests that judgment be entered in their favor and against defendants for:

(a) Statutory damages pursuant to 15 U.S.C. 1692k;

(b) Costs and reasonable attorney fees pursuant to 15 U.S.C. 1692k;

(c) A right to a trial by jury;

(d) For such other and further relief as to this Court seems just and proper.

## COUNT II
### 15 U.S.C. 1692e(2)(A), e(5), e(10)

18. Plaintiff repeats and reiterates allegations in paragraphs 1-17 above, as if fully set forth herein.

19. Defendants threatened to place derogatory information on

plaintiff's credit report, even though said derogatory information and too old to legally be placed on a credit report pursuant to the time limitations for reporting derogatory information on a credit report pursuant to the Fair Credit Reporting Act (15 U.S.C. 1681 et. seq.).

20. Threatening to take action that cannot be legally taken, namely, threatening to place derogatory remarks on a credit report regarding information which exceeds limitations of the Fair Credit Reporting Act requirement (15 U.S.C. 1681 et. seq.), violates 15 U.S.C. 1692e(2)(A), as it misrepresents the character and amount of the debt.

21. Threatening to take action that cannot be legally taken, namely, threatening to place derogatory remarks on a credit report regarding information which exceeds limitations of the Fair Credit Reporting Act requirement (15 U.S.C. 1681 et. seq.), violates 15 U.S.C. 1692e(5), as it represents a threat that cannot be taken in accordance with the rules of placing antiquated information on a credit report.

22. Threatening to take action that cannot be legally taken, namely, threatening to place derogatory remarks on a credit report regarding information which exceeds limitations of the Fair Credit Reporting Act requirement (15 U.S.C. 1681 et. seq.), violates 15 U.S.C. 1692e(10), as it is the use of a false and deceptive means to attempt to collect a debt.

WHEREFORE, as to Count II, plaintiffs respectfully requests that judgment be entered in their favor and against defendants for:

(a) Statutory damages pursuant to 15 U.S.C. 1692k;

(b) Costs and reasonable attorney fees pursuant to 15 U.S.C. 1692k;

(c) A right to a trial by jury;

(d) For such other and further relief as to this Court seems just and proper.

## COUNT III
### 15 U.S.C. 1692f(2)

23. Plaintiff repeats and reiterates allegations in paragraphs 1-22 above, as if fully set forth herein.

24. Holding funds and a post dated check for more than five days is a violation of 1692f(2).

WHEREFORE, as to Count III, plaintiff respectfully requests that judgment be entered in their favor and against defendants for:

(a) Statutory damages pursuant to 15 U.S.C. 1692k;

(b) Costs and reasonable attorney fees pursuant to 15 U.S.C. 1692k;

(c) A right to a trial by jury;

(d) For such other and further relief as to this Court seems just and proper.

## COUNT IV
### 15 U.S.C. 1692g

25. Plaintiff repeats and reiterates allegations in paragraphs 1-24 above, as if fully set forth herein.

26. At all times herein, defendants failed to provide the verification of debt as provided in 15 U.S.C. 1692g.

WHEREFORE, as to Count V, plaintiff respectfully requests that judgment be entered in their favor and against defendants for:

(a) Statutory damages pursuant to 15 U.S.C. 1692k;

(b) Costs and reasonable attorney fees pursuant to 15 U.S.C. 1692k;

(c) A right to a trial by jury;

(d) For such other and further relief as to this Court seems just and proper.

Respectfully submitted,

RICHARD L. DIMAGGIO
Attorney for plaintiff
P.O. Box 104
Clifton Park, New York 12065

## SAMPLE #5
### Communication with Third Parties, Extreme Harassment

UNITED STATES DISTRICT COURT
DISTRICT OF
_____

YOU,

Plaintiff,

Index No.

-against-

JURY DEMAND

THEM Collections Group,

COMPLAINT

Defendant.
_____

1. Plaintiff, YOU, brings this action for redress of Defendants violations of the Fair Debt Collection Practices Act, 15 U.S.C. 1692 et. seq. (hereinafter "FDCPA"). Defendants, by and through their employees, harassed and threatened plaintiff through intimidating and hateful remarks and messages left to plaintiff's colleagues at work and to plaintiff.

### JURISDICTION

2. Jurisdiction is vested in this Court pursuant to 15 U.S.C. 1692k(d) and 28 U.S.C. 1337.

### PARTIES

3. Plaintiff, YOU, is a natural person residing at Water Ave., Anywhere, NY.

4. The defendant, THEM Collections Group, is a foreign corporation and a debt collector, and maintains a place of business in Chicago, IL.

### FACTUAL ALLEGATIONS

5. This case arises out of nonpayment of a credit card in plaintiff's name, to wit, a BBBB account. Upon information and belief, BBBB sold the account to FFFF Acquisition, LLC, on or about July 28th, 2000.

6. Sherman Acquisition referred the account to THEM defendants herein, for debt collection. Those debt collection attempts by THEM, form the nexus of this instant litigation.

7. Defendants called plaintiff many times at work. Plaintiff repeatedly told defendants not to call her at work, that work is an inconvenient time to be contacted.

8. Despite the information, defendants called plaintiff repeatedly at work at her place of employment.

9. What occurred during the course of these phone calls to plaintiff and plaintiff's colleagues ripens into a course of conduct and debt collection activities which was meant to threaten, scare, belittle, and cause extreme emotional distress.

10. During the conversations, a "Mr. W—", a debt collector who works for defendant, would tell plaintiff that she had "one hour to pay the debt—or else."

11. W— would then call plaintiff's colleagues and ask them if "they could identify her," and inquire what time plaintiff would be leaving the building to go home.

12. Attached hereto as Exhibit "A" is a true and just copy of a message to plaintiff dated February 4th, 2000, where W— inquired if plaintiff's supervisor could identify her, and left the message to tell plaintiff "good luck."

13. The clear import of the language was that defendants were threatening plaintiff when she left her building and were stalking her for the purpose of causing her physical harm.

14. Defendants discussed the debt with plaintiff's colleagues.

15. Defendants told plaintiff she had "an hour" to pay "or else."

16. Other times, defendants told plaintiff she had "24 hours to pay."

17. Defendants would repeatedly scream at plaintiff over the phone, so loudly as to cause plaintiff to hold the phone far away from her ear.

18. The insinuations of threats of physical harm to plaintiff became so severe, plaintiff's colleagues wanted her to get an escort to her car because they were afraid for her.

19. The majority of the acts herein described were committed by a Mr. M—, a Mr. W—, and a Mr. J—.

20. At one time, a caller screamed at plaintiff, "I'm not putting up with your shit anymore."

21. That the callers herein, and each of them, at all times, were employees of the defendant and were working under their care, custody, control, and supervision, and were acting within the scope of their employment.

22. That the acts herein described were meant and intended to cause plaintiff severe emotional distress, and did cause plaintiff severe emotional distress, anxiety, sleeplessness, and stress.

## COUNT I
### 15 U.S.C. 1692 et. seq. 1692c(a)(1), 1692c(a)(3), 1692c(b), 1692d, 1692e

23. Plaintiff repeats and reiterates allegations in paragraphs 1-22 above, as if fully set forth herein.

24. Contacting plaintiff at work, at a place where the collector knows is inconvenient, is a violation of 1692c.

25. Contacting plaintiff at work, at a place where the collector knows is inconvenient, and where the collector knows that the employer prohibits such communication, is a violation of 1692c(a)(3).

26. Contacting plaintiff after being requested not to is a violation of 1692c(c).

27. Calling plaintiff, and screaming at her, and using obscenities, is a violation of 1692d, and is meant to harass and abuse plaintiff into paying a debt.

28. The facts herein alleged constitute a false and misleading attempt to collect a debt, in violation of 1692e.

29. The facts herein alleged constitute an unfair practice, and is in violation of 1692f.

30. That all said acts were done intentionally, willfully and maliciously.

31. That the plaintiff herein suffered emotional distress, anxiety and humiliation and is entitled to punitive damages and actual damages.

WHEREFORE, as to Count I, plaintiff respectfully requests that judgment be entered in her favor and against defendants for:

(a) Statutory damages pursuant to 15 U.S.C. 1692k;

(b) Costs and reasonable attorney fees pursuant to 15 U.S.C. 1692k;

(c) Emotional distress (actual damages) of $1,000,000;

(d) A right to a trial by jury;

(e) For such other and further relief as to this Court seems just and proper.

## COUNT II
## INTENTIONAL INFLICTION OF EMOTIONAL DISTRESS

32. Plaintiff repeats and reiterates allegations in paragraphs 1-31 above, as fully set forth herein.

33. The acts herein described were intended and meant to cause plaintiff emotional distress, and plaintiff, as a direct and proximate cause of such acts, did suffer from extreme emotional distress.

34. That the clear import of the words and action herein described, including but not limited to the threat and insinuation of physical violence, were made willfully and maliciously and with the intent to make plaintiff fear for her life.

WHEREFORE, as to Count II, plaintiff respectfully requests that judgment be entered in her favor and against defendants for:

(a) Punitive damages of $5,000,000;

(b) Emotional distress of $1,000,000;

(c) A right to a trial by jury;

(d) For such other and further relief as to this Court seems just and proper.

Respectfully submitted,

RICHARD L. DIMAGGIO
Attorney for plaintiff
1009 London Square Drive
Clifton Park, New York 12065

1. *Barasch v. Pa. Public Utility Commission,* 576 A.2d 79 (Pa. Commonwealth Ct).

2. 47 C.F.R. 64.1601(b)(1996.

3. *Macarz v. Transworld Systems, Inc.,* 26 F. Supp.2d 368, 372 (D. Conn. 1998), *citing Gaetano v. Payco of Wisconsin,* Inc., 774 F. Supp. 1404, 1410. (D. Conn. 1990), quoting in turn, S. Rep. No. 382, 95th Cong. 2d Sess. 4, reprinted in 1977 U.S. Code Cong. & Admin. News 1695, 1699.

4. *Jang v. A.M. Miller and Assoc.,* 122 F. 3d 480, 483 (7th Cir. 1997) citing 15 U.S.C. 1692g(b).

5. *Smith v. Transworld Systems,* 953 F. 2d 1025 (6th Cir. 1992).

6. *Rabideau v. Management Adjustment Bureau* 805 F. Supp. 1086, 1092 (W.D.N.Y. 1992).

7. *Russell v. Equifax,* 74 F.3d 30 (1996).

8. *United States v. Central Adjustment Bureau, Inc.,* 667 F. Supp. 370 (N.D.Tex 1986), *affirmed,* 823 F. 2d 880 (5th Cir. 1987).

9. *Bingham v. Collection Bureau, Inc.,* 505 F. Supp. 864 (D.N.D. 1981).

10. *Bingham v. Collection Bureau, Inc.,* 505 F. Supp. 864 (D.N.D. 1981).

11. *Bently v. Great Lakes Collections Bureau,* 6 F.3d 60 (U.S. Ct. App. 2d Cir. 1993); *Pipiles v. Credit Bureau of Lockport, Inc.,* 886 F. 2d 22 (U.S. Ct. App. 2d Cir. 1989); *Tsenes v. Tran-Continental Credit ad Collection Corp.,* 892 F. Supp. 461 (2d. Cir. 1995).

12. *Clomon v. Jackson,* 988 F. 2d 1314 (U.S. Ct. App. 2d. Cir.).

13. *Rivera v. Bank One,* 145 F.R.D. 614 (D. Puerto Rico, 1993). *See also, Ditty v. Checkrite, LTD., Inc.,* 973 F. Supp. 1320, 1331 (D. Utah 1997). "While Checkrite may have had some legitimate business purpose for making such communications, it is clear that the practice was also designed to provide Checkrite with additional leverage in collecting the debts created by plaintiff's dishonored checks."; *In re Sommersdorf,* 139 B.R. 700, 701 (Bkr. S.D. Ohio, 1991).

14. *Gray-Mapp v. Sherman,* 100 F. Supp. 2d. 810 (N.D. Ill 2000).

15. *Molloy v. Primus Automotive Financial Services,* 247 B.R. 804; 2000 Lexis 7277. On page 821, the court states: "Allowing a bankrupt debtor to assert an FDCPA claim could potentially undermine the Bankruptcy Code's specific provisions for administration of the debtor's estate. Here, in contrast, plaintiff's FDCPA claim is based solely on Primus' alleged debt collection activities outside of and in disregard of the bankruptcy proceeding. Moreover, plaintiff has been discharged from her bankruptcy, so there is no danger that allowing her to bring a claim under the FDCPA would interfere with the administration of her bankruptcy. Inasmuch as the FDCPA's purpose is to prevent a bankruptcy, a debtor who has been discharged is still entitled to the Act's protection. For these reasons, the Court does not find the authorities cited by defendant persuasive." The case *Wagner v. Ocwen,* 2000 U.S. Dist. Lexis 12463, also holds that the FDCPA is not preempted by the Bankruptcy Code.

16. *11 U.S.C. 524* states, in part, that a bankruptcy discharge, " . . . operates as an injunction against the commencement or continuation of an action, the employment of process, or an act, to collect, recover or offset any such debt as a personal liability of the debtor, whether or not discharge of such debt is waived."

17. *See Legislative History, 11 U.S.C. 524.* "Discharge carries with it an injunction against debt collection efforts. The injunction imposed by 524(a)(2) is intentionally broad in scope and is intended to preclude virtually all actions by a creditor to collect personally from the debtor."

18. H.R. Rep. No. 595, 95th Cong., 1st Sess. 363-64 (1977); S. Rep. No. 989, 95th Cong., 2d Sess. 80 (1978) 524, prohibits any act whatsoever to collect on a debt discharged in bankruptcy.